T0023203

"To be on the left, one requires possession of a quixotic sense of romanticism. From the Paris Commune to the Spanish Civil War, Che, the Black Panthers and striking workers — we have always been inspired by sacrificial 'heroes'. The old macho idea of 'great men of history' and the millenarian fashion for non-hierarchal horizontalism killed off the need for such figures. Sorry, it's a fact that in the twenty-first century we are in need of new charismatic leaders, heroes even. This book is an unashamed celebration of the everyday heroic. Read and be inspired."

— **BOBBY GILLESPIE**

THE REPEATER BOOK OF **HEROISM**

Published by Repeater Books

An imprint of Watkins Media Ltd

Unit 11 Shepperton House

89-93 Shepperton Road

London

N1 3DF

United Kingdom

www.repeaterbooks.com

A Repeater Books hardback original 2022

1

Distributed in the United States by Random House, Inc., New York.

Copyright © Repeater Books 2022

ISBN: 9781914420023

Ebook ISBN: 9781914420030

All rights reserved. No part of this publication may be reproduced, stored in a retrieval system, or transmitted, in any form or by any means, electronic, mechanical, photocopying, recording or otherwise, without the prior permission of the publishers.

This book is sold subject to the condition that it shall not, by way of trade or otherwise, be lent, resold, hired out or otherwise circulated without the publisher's prior consent in any form of binding or cover other than that in which it is published and without a similar condition including this condition being imposed on the subsequent purchaser.

Printed and bound in the United Kingdom by TJ Books Ltd

THE REPEATER BOOK OF **HEROISM**

EDITED BY **TARIQ GODDARD** & **ALEX NIVEN**

ILLUSTRATIONS BY **CHRISTIANA SPENS**

For Dawn Foster, Repeater hero number 1

CONTENTS

INTRODUCTION / TARIQ GODDARD & ALEX NIVEN

For the longest time, heroes and heroism have had a bad press. For a host of reasons — World War II perhaps, or postmodernism, or punk — the ancient art of glorifying a single human being has, for at least half a century, been one of the biggest taboos in almost every discourse going. "Putting someone up on a pedestal" has become something you *definitely do not do under any circumstances* — the suggestion itself synonymous with a proscribed desire to rate, categorise and rank.

In practice, of course, this new decorum has arisen at the same time as inequality between individuals has notably failed to disappear. Meanwhile, a new kind of mythic figure has thrived as never before. In the bleak dreamscape of twenty-first-century capitalism, "icons", "influencers" and "curators" are perfectly acceptable. Similarly, "celebrities" and "celebrity culture" (in sport, art, fashion and politics) are part of the lifeblood of an increasingly depraved system. Quasi-authoritarian leaders like Trump, Orbán, Modi and Bolsonaro (and, lower down the food chain, desperate end-of-the-pier turns like Johnson and Farage) have dominated later neoliberalism, for all their bogus claims about being figureheads of a popular backlash against the status quo.

In this context, is there any room at all for the old-fangled, moth-eaten figure of the hero — or at least the related, but not necessarily insuperable concept of heroism?

The deeper reasons for the contemporary left's misgivings about heroism are historically understandable. An outlook

1

that prizes equality and distrusts meritocracy might wonder what it has to learn from heroism per se. Yet such scepticism is as much a symptom of political defeat as it is sound egalitarian sense. Fifty years ago, the entries in a collection like this would have chosen themselves: Marx, Engels, Trotsky and Mao, or perhaps Cleaver, Castro, Guevara and possibly even Baader, a verifiable rollcall of revolutionary virility. The belief that a radical leader should want to overthrow society and establish a new order (an idea most prevalent in the campuses of the North Atlantic democracies), held enormous aesthetic and social, if not always political, traction.

However, the political failure of authoritarian socialism, the emphasis on human rights and turn against violence as an effective way of achieving one's political goals felled this article of faith and broke the pantheon apart, discrediting some of its luminaries and rendering others, at best, irrelevant. A new consensus saw all leaders, even good ones, as necessarily having blood on their hands, and heroism itself as a destructive stance, more likely to encourage macho posturing than creative invention. By abandoning armed revolution, the dictatorship of the proletariat and a vanguardist leadership, the left junked those features most closely associated with them — individual personality cults, elitism and exceptionalism in general — all of which have become the province of the right.

Having lost the external signifiers of heroism, the next step was to deprive it of its driving forces — inspiration and appeals to raw feeling, which as essentialist enablers, theological anachronisms or bourgeois constructs, were now as toxic as bravery, courage, sacrifice and fortitude. Instead of these hoary old platitudes, new and ever more exacting standards of perfect(ly moral) behaviour were required for a person to be worthy of unordinary admiration. In its most extreme form, this variety of resentment used criteria the progressive left would traditionally have avoided: that a person should be judged by the worst thing they have ever done and not the best, that ontological redemption, the ability to create something good or of utility even when otherwise morally compromised, was a form of cheating and therefore worthy of disqualification. Against such odds, heroism could not possibly survive, and its replacements, however noble, worthy or deconstructive, were simply not *heroic* enough to fulfil its old functions.

The essays in this book are all in some way based on the premise that a hero is, in spite of everything, something to be. To be clear, in wishing to make the case for the legitimacy of heroism as an idea and rallying cry in the twenty-first century, we are not trying to resuscitate reactionary, outdated and discredited forms of hero-worship. In 1841, at the start of the Victorian era, the Scottish historian Thomas Carlyle published *On Heroes, Hero-Worship, and the Heroic in History*. Carlyle's book was in the main a sinister development, which kick-started a modern tradition of dealing with heroes and the heroic that would lead to some very dark places indeed. In making a passionate case for a "Great Man" theory of human history, *On Heroes* opened the door to all manner of ethical evils, from the notion of male greatness to the forms of imperialist and authoritarian domination which follow from a belief that, as Carlyle put it: "great men are the commissioned guides of mankind, who rule their fellows". It is no wonder that the concept of an all-powerful *Übermensch* was later developed and adopted by twentieth-century fascist ideologues, who took Carlyle's argument as their food and drink.

But while acknowledging the ultimate failure and degradation of the nineteenth-century cult of the hero, and the validity of some of the contemporary left's hostility to the idea, we must now, in our changed, changing world, have the courage and the intelligence to try to recover more powerful, more subtle, more loving forms of heroism, or else surrender this ground forever to the right.

The reader can take it as given that none of the contributors to this book think that calling someone "a hero" or identifying instances of human beings acting heroically means that we should go in search of a twenty-first-century version of the *Übermensch*. Instead, as you will see as you read the following essays, the writers assembled here — all of whom have previously had work published with the quixotic, idealistic project that is Repeater Books — are united in a belief that recovering the heroic is a vital precondition of collective action (and therefore also socialism, or whatever term you want to apply to the radical dream of an alternative to our present, individualist system which enslaves individuals).

In the pages that follow, we see how a fierce, even absurd (but never excessive) belief in the extraordinary capabilities of another human being has acted as an important moment in the life of each of the writers here. The entries in this book often read as much as personal confessions as they do eulogies to others. By encouraging our writers to eschew those worthy names who often make feature on lists of the greatest and best, we hope to emphasise how heroism can be found in the unlikeliest and most egoless of lives, often by those who simply existed in and of themselves, without a thought for greatness or glory.

We also see how it is possible — even vital — to hold a dual reality in our minds: that our fellow human beings may be flawed in all kinds of profound ways, but that the possibility of heroism is always within reach for even the most conflicted and compromised of individuals. Sneering at "cancel culture" has become one of the favourite forms of attack for the right over the last few years — a way of trying to undermine legitimate forms of censure, criticism and debate which it does not like. Nevertheless, the highly politicised and fragmentary culture of the twenty-first century (not to mention the paranoid atmosphere of social media) has fed the left's tendency towards moral censure, which judges individuals by way of a complex set of shifting ideological criteria, and which can leave little room for the possibility that someone who has once done or said something ethically dubious might still be capable of being — in a significant sense — a hero.

This attempt to recover heroism from the jaws of our enemies is at the heart of the Repeater Books project — and it is the unifying principle which links together the disparate pieces of writing in the book you are holding in your hands. A heroic act is literally timeless, and always an example to us, however much the individual responsible for it may degenerate and fail to live up to their finest hour(s). In 1976, John Lydon said: "I don't have any heroes; they're all useless." He was right: your heroes do let you down. They have to, because they are human. But by being so they invite us to fail better. More importantly, perhaps, the flawed, human side of heroism invites each new generation to replace the last constellation of stars with newer, more intricate embodiments of grandeur and grace.

JENNIFER ANISTON / ALEX NIVEN

The 1990s were a decade of endings. End of the century, end of the millennium, end of the Cold War. The post-war counterculture (pop music and poetry spliced with radical politics) faded out and morphed finally into hipsterdom, its parodic opposite. At the same time, post-war social democracy — to say nothing of actually-existing socialism — finally gave up the ghost and conceded that the global neoliberal empire was, for the moment, unassailable. For Francis Fukuyama, famously and hyperbolically, this was the end of history itself.

But when compared to the 2020s — our own anxious and enfeebled decade — the 1990s seem with hindsight to have been a time of rare youthful confidence. A defining narrative of recent years has been the gradual, tragic disempowerment of the young, so that so-called millennials and zoomers (people born after circa 1980) have become a relatively impoverished minority without much leverage over the power structures of Western society and politics. My generation and its successor are interminably caught in a sort of historical hiatus. For the most part, we can only look backward as we search for existential sustenance and inspiration.

From the vantage point of the present, the end of the twentieth century seems like the last moment when the West underwent genuine — if partial and ambiguous — socio-political renewal. The mass cultural markers of this last generational takeover are gathered together in the familiar pantheon of 1990s popular art — *Friends*, Oasis, the Spice Girls, *This Life*, *Pulp Fiction*, the Premier League. For all their variety (and deep moral ambivalence), these touchstones almost all convey a strong sense of conviction, vitality and abandon, of the kind that is at the forefront in any period when a new historical cohort arrives to lay claim to its long-hoped-for majority.

For enough young people to make a sweeping generalisation on the subject sort of excusable, the 1990s were a time of making it now, of coming out off the sidelines, of finally finding something worth living for and telling the world what you really, *really* wanted. We might now look back on this period with a mixture of nostalgia, embarrassment and distaste. But whatever its ethical and ideological complications, there is no doubt that 1990s culture said what it wanted to say and did so pretty forcibly.

Perhaps, at the most basic level, this is what heroism is. Heroes are not cautious. They do not — if they are not like Hamlet, the first real anti-hero — split hairs in agonising about their place in the world. Neither do they appear to spend much time worrying about past and future, in spite of the fact that it is posterity that will eventually sustain them. A hero is a human being who is remembered for taking possession of the *now*. History gives heroes a chance, and they have the gall and good fortune to take it.

Nowadays, the whole basis of contemporary life seems to disavow the possibility of the hero, even as it has created ample space for the hero's evil twin, the celebrity, to become hegemonic. There are basic historical reasons for this shift. I don't want to sound like an avowed Nietzschean, but it seems fairly self-evident that one of the main things we have to reckon with, in the post-1990s era, is a sort of hyper-anxious, hyper-conscious rationality, which makes the emergence of authentic hero figures very difficult, if not impossible, to imagine.

The twenty-first-century world spirit, which has emerged in the absence of any really confident iteration of newness and nowness, is defined above all by a reticence bordering on hopelessness. The twenty-first-century young are over-educated, over-worked (or under-employed) and terminally insecure. Partly because of this harsh socio-economic backdrop, they have been unable to move beyond the deconstructive postures which defined the preceding era, even as they have largely failed to carry over the *jouissance* which made late-twentieth-century relativism occasionally tolerable. Millennials and zoomers have been barred from taking possession of their historical moment. As a result, and in spite of their immense talents and strenuous labours, they cannot find a way to partake of the heroism which might follow from an assured seizure of *au courant* social and political power.

But what we do have, in our exhausted, uncertain present tense, is a newly confident political morality — and for the most part, it is a righteous one. In stark contrast to the post-historical, apolitical, even outright amoral 1990s, in the early decades of the twenty-first century we have seen a revival of political consciousness which has largely exceeded the confines of sectional divisions to become something like a global movement proper — even if the continued dominance of older demographics has thus far blunted and stifled the ability of that movement to make actual political inroads.

The deepening class awareness first signalled by the Occupy movement's "We are the 99%" rallying cry of the early 2010s; the joyous liberation of gender typologies which has become a counterculture in itself over the last five years or so; the determined anti-racism of the Black Lives Matter vanguard and its offshoots; and the increasingly popular cause of radical ecology: all point to a revival and foregrounding of political militancy which might just, if it can be successfully harnessed and implemented, produce a revolutionary crossover moment in the next quarter century (that is, if climate change does not destroy much of the world first).

But the fundamental vulnerability of what the political theorist Keir Milburn calls "Generation Left" continually threatens to cut off its oxygen supply and prevent it from making any concrete popular gains. In a controversial, now infamous essay of late 2013, the late Repeater founder (and hero) Mark Fisher created an exaggerated metaphor for the deconstructive, hyper-moralistic instincts of the contemporary left in the form of the "Vampire's Castle". According to Fisher, this is a zone of mainly online left discourse, which "seeks to corral people back into identi-camps, where they are forever defined in the terms set by dominant power, crippled by self-consciousness and isolated by a logic of solipsism".

In keeping with its author's manic side, "Exiting the Vampire Castle" was chaotic and excessive in style, especially in an overlong and eccentric second half. Nevertheless, the essential point made in Fisher's essay — that twenty-first-century radicals are "crippled by self-consciousness" and "isolated by solipsism" — and thereby set against one another in a way that suits the global political system pretty well — is a useful and pithy diagnosis of our contemporary malaise.

For Fisher, the internecine squabbling and "call-out culture" which has beset the modern left is partly an expression of the internet's internal procedural logic, which makes "left-wing Twitter" a site of "witch-hunting moralism", "snarky resentment" and even frequent bullying. But as well as this surface context, we should delve deeper as we seek to understand why we have thus far been unable to muster any really lasting sense of optimism, belief and momentum behind the twenty-first-century radical campaign.

As well as more local explanations, it seems clear that a large part of the reason for the contemporary left's failure of nerve — or rather, its inability to rise above acute nervousness in the first place — is its basic lack of social empowerment, which has prevented it from entering an important cultural space: that magic-zone of freeing acceptance of comradely difference that is the true hallmark of a historical movement in the ascendant. Pacified by marginality, overwork, economic hardship and sheer, rational dysphoria and dread, the descent into hair-splitting inward critique and brooding inaction which has characterised the post-1990s (post-)counterculture is predictable.

How then to flip the switch? I do not pretend to have any really programmatic or practical answers. But it seems fairly obvious to me that a small, meaningful part of the solution to the problem of contemporary left paralysis will lie in an energetic recovery of what might, for want of a better word, be called heroism. Believing in the essential, remarkable, imperfect goodness of fellow travellers in one's own embattled cohort — and not collapsing the proverbial ton of bricks on anyone who briefly and innocuously strays from ideological decorum — would be a very good starting point in this regard.

But probably it will take a much greater feat of imaginative daring — not to mention objective luck — if we are to have any hope at all of turning the cart around and avoiding catastrophe, let alone introducing the basic political reforms our withered, fatally unequal society so desperately needs. Maybe, in order to truly succeed, we will need to find a way of pressing pause on self-criticism and even rationality itself for a while. Maybe, looking at our comrades with an exaggerated sense of confidence, optimism and encouragement, rather than perpetually vetting them for minor foibles, will create an environment in which the rise of heroes capable of leading the twenty-first-century left becomes a little more likely (and yes, we do need leaders of some kind). All we can do is give it our best shot, and hope that history meets us halfway, in providing the conditions necessary for a new Now to slowly or suddenly emerge.

Until then, I am going to gesture finally, bathetically, and more or less arbitrarily, at Jennifer Aniston as an example of what heroism means to me. In addition to being the greatest comic actor of her age, she communicates a couple of basic, forceful messages which encapsulate some of the things I have been trying to articulate in this piece of writing.

Outside of the quiet feminist undertow to her narrative, Aniston ticks very few moral-ideological boxes. Nevertheless, she is a powerful reminder of the last really major moment of cultural juvenescence we can draw inspiration from: a 1990s interlude in which, for all its flaws, there was an empowering sense of belief, tolerance and acceptance in the air — a mood which at times enabled people to move beyond nuance and achieve a kind of fleeting historical grandeur.

As we hold out for heroes of our own, we could do a lot worse than look back on the elegant, funny, endlessly dignified example of Jennifer Aniston — an avatar of her age, and the *de facto* leader of a group of friends coming into their own.

GIORDANO BRUNO / PETER FLEMING

Ash Wednesday, 17 February 1600. A naked man —
bloodied and exhausted — sits on a mule slowly winding
its way through the cobblestoned streets of the old city.
The gathering crowd understood this was no ordinary
heretic. Some feared the sorcery he might summon and
kept a safe distance. Others looked away in silent respect.
Upon arriving at the Campo, the ex-priest and brilliant
cosmologist Giordano Bruno was frog-marched to the pyre
and had his legs tied before being hoisted upside down at
the stake. The Inquisition had gagged him to avoid any
last-minute outbursts. If his written words were dangerous
— all his books were on the *Index Librorum Prohibitorum* —
then his tongue was doubly so. A crucifix was presented
for him to kiss and Bruno turned away in disgust. After the
tinder was lit his hair, head and neck were soon consumed
by flame. The agonising moans subsided and the heretic
was reduced to ash.

Visiting Rome in 2010, I called on a friend who helped run
a neighbourhood collective. It was a wonderful space, rent-
free and occupied. Even better, they were having a party.
After much wine, the evening grew late and I mentioned
my pilgrimage to Campo de' Fiori the next morning. "Why
don't we go now?" my friend smiled, pointing to his Vespa.
Next we were speeding through the narrow streets of that
labyrinthine city, me clinging to dear life on the back of
the scooter. Entering the Campo we approached the statue
of Bruno standing at its centre. "There he is," my friend

whispered. "And up there," he pointed to a window on the upper-most corner of a large building, "the Inquisitors watched."

My fascination with Bruno began in childhood. When I was six or seven years old, feeling unwell and off from school, my mother gave me one of her art history books to browse. I came across an etching or engraving — I cannot quite remember — of a man whose youthful appearance surprised me. "That's the radical stargazer," my mother said, looking over my shoulder. Later on in my early teens I developed a strong interest in astronomy, and my mother bought a cheap reflector telescope. We spent long summer evenings exploring the beautiful night sky of the Southern Hemisphere. The dark and mysterious mists of Eta Carina. The vast star clouds of Sagittarius and the Trifid Nebular. The Southern Cross with its delicate Jewell Box star cluster. The Magellanic Clouds orbiting the Milky Way some 200,000 lightyears away.

Bruno is often remembered as a recalcitrant religious figure. But his cosmological theories are what truly enraged the papal authorities because they unseated almost everything — not just morality and society but the natural world too, all of which were deeply entwined in late-Renaissance Europe. Bruno is the archetypal freethinker, one so uncompromising that even *he* seemed shocked by the words emanating from his mouth. How could you say *that*? Writing was his key medium, however. It too was like an external force, almost machinic and beyond his control. Bruno simply had to write — apostolic tracts, philosophy, meditations on astronomy, comedies, plays, etc. — and the Printing Revolution added fuel to the fire of an already incendiary mind.

Born near Naples in 1548, Bruno joined the Dominican order at the age of seventeen. He then became renowned for two things. First, his astonishing memory — Bruno developed an ingenious mnemonic system (based upon concentric thought-wheels) that yielded breath-taking feats of recall. Some suggested that no mortal could do this and witchcraft must be at play. And second, Bruno immediately started challenging the orthodoxy of the order, openly broaching theological controversies that none dared mention. When an annotated copy of Erasmus' banned writings were discovered in the monastery loos, the Inquisition opened a file on Bruno and he fled.

He wandered Europe for years in search of work as a scholar and teacher, discarding his priestly garb and disappearing into the crowd. Bruno travelled to northern Italy and then Geneva where he found employment as a proofreader and dabbled in Calvinism. But he couldn't keep his mouth shut. After criticising a local professor, he left Geneva to take a doctorate at Toulouse and then a position in Paris. Bruno's fame grew in France due to his amazing memory, even gaining an audience with Henry III. His confidence also grew. Upon visiting Oxford University, Bruno concluded that zero original thought was happening there. But while in England he did manage to publish his major cosmological works, including *De la causa, principio et uno* (*On Cause, Principle and Unity*), *De l'infinito, universo et mondi* (*On the Infinite, Universe and Worlds*) and *La cena de le ceneri* (*The Ash Wednesday Supper*). Controversy predictably followed and Bruno returned to Paris, where the climate had soured significantly. He travelled to Germany and then Prague. Finally, Bruno was enticed back to Italy for a teaching position. But his disgruntled patron — Bruno had an uncanny gift for offending people in authority — denounced him to the Inquisition and he was arrested.

Bruno's biography is integral to his thinking. He followed a nomadic, even fugitive way of life that imbued his thought too. No one needs a better memory than a man on the run. The exiled scholar never settled and required no geographical centre. Indeed, *settlement*, with all of its imperial connotations, repelled Bruno (unlike the academic norm later inaugurated by Kant, who never strayed far from his birthplace and followed a timepiece way of life).

This centreless and peripatetic texture of Bruno's life shaped his heterodox ideas in other ways, particularly his cosmological meditations. He openly supported Copernicus' heliocentric theory, uprooting the Ptolemaic doctrine of a fixed Earth sitting at the heart of a closed universe. Copernicus placed the sun at the centre instead, with the Earth and stars revolving on celestial spheres. Bruno went further. Perhaps the sun wasn't the centre of the universe either. What if there were innumerable suns, all of which have planets revolving around them, some even teeming with life? He got that idea from Nicholas of Cusa but saw it through to its logical conclusion. The universe is centreless and ultimately infinite, making mankind an insignificant speck in an endless abyss. Bruno clearly knew what he was doing. Christianity relied on an immoveable, crowning core to function and he smashed it into countless fragments. Only in that multitude of fragments might we sense God, Bruno averred, in both the infinitesimal and infinite, those gentle clouds slowly moving across the sky, that lone spider's web in a forgotten corner of the copse.

For the Roman Inquisition, this was as good as saying that God doesn't exist and the Holy Scriptures are an elaborate fable concocted by clever animals on a pointless planet. But Bruno was not quite an atheist or pantheist. He most likely followed an apophatic creed (*via negativa*), making him more of a pandeist. In any case, when Inquisitor Cardinal Bellarmine (who was beatified in 1923) demanded a full recantation, Bruno refused. The trial concluded with the death sentence and Bruno's famous retort, "*Maiori forsan cum timore sententiam in me fertis quam ego accipiam*" ("Perchance you pronounce this sentence against me with greater fear than I receive it"). In other words, when power resorts to violence, particularly of the most egregious kind, it betrays a fatal weakness and signals its imminent demise.

There's been much debate about whether Bruno was burned at the stake because of his theological views (making him a garden variety "witch" like all the others) or his ground-breaking cosmology (making him a so-called "martyr" of science and free speech). The Inquisition's formal list of charges is now lost. However, a letter written by a witness to the immolation — one Gaspar Schoppe — says the first indictment read was "that there's a countless amount of Worlds". This certainly informed the other charges, like "Christ is not god", etc.

Does this make Bruno a martyr of science? "Martyr" is the wrong word, given its doctrinal connotations — especially sacrifice — and unduly romanticises the issue. Bruno simply faced an impossible dilemma. Either recant and live in a world without a universe (which would be like inhabiting a cupboard for Bruno), or die a horrible death. The crucial point is this, however. Bruno didn't choose to die, which would indeed make him a martyr. Death instead somehow chose him. He thus honoured one of the most difficult ethical precepts we know: be worthy of what happens to you. In light of his death and the imprisonment of Galileo (who did indeed recant), the nascent scientific community realised that Copernicus was probably worth reading closely. The universe was nearly lost and Bruno did his part in saving it, one of the few domains that will never be touched by the madness of man. Studying super-collapsed neutron stars or the bizarre "V381 Nor" quasar is practically useless to the state, corporations and financial markets. Yet it represents the highest order of human knowledge and profoundly disturbs the meaning of existence and society.

I never got to tell my mother how much those summer nights at the telescope meant to me. It's strange. Whenever I think of her now, it's as she was back then, in the mid-1980s. A vibrant and brave woman, teaching me the constellations and working through the star atlas. Adulthood inevitably arrives under different skies. I packed my bags the night before. Toothbrush and jeans. Weeping and hugs. The airport taxi parked out front. I looked back one more time. And left.

DORA / JOY WHITE

It seems strange to offer up a hero who you only met in person twice, but I have solid reasons for doing so. My grandmother Dora was a traveller, she possessed a kind and caring spirit that went beyond her immediate family. She had a strong sense of community, she made sure that what little they had was shared. All of the children in her care went to school no matter the financial hardship, and no one went hungry. And although this may seem low on the heroic scale, making this happen in a British colony, which built its wealth and boosted industrial advance from enslaving people as property,[1] is no mean feat.

Dora had a powerful work ethic, she told me about going to Coronation market in Kingston to sell produce. A journey of some fifty miles, it would take many hours to get there, particularly at that time when transport was scarce and the roads were treacherous.

---

1 I have drawn on the data in Gisela Eisner's book, which looks at economic growth in Jamaica from 1830-1930. It outlines in gruesome detail how, using slave labour, Jamaica was run as a sugar-growing, plantation economy for the benefit and profit of largely absentee British owners. Post-emancipation, an apprenticeship system was in place until 1838; after that, former slaves could become small-scale cultivators, buying or renting parcels of usually undesirable land. See: Gisela Eisner, *Jamaica, 1830-1930: A Study in Economic Growth*. Westport, Conn: Praeger, 1974.

We met for the first time in extraordinary circumstances, on my first visit to Jamaica in 1988, shortly before Hurricane Gilbert struck.[2] I was the last grandchild that she met in person. Up until that point, I only knew her from the contents of the flimsy blue airmail letters that would arrive at regular intervals. These letters brought news from a place that my parents called "back home".

What you do need to know is that Dorell "Dora" Gertrude Ricketts was born in Jamaica in 1905. In the early 1920s she travelled to Cuba with my grandad Robert. I'm not sure of the exact date but Robert's travel document for Cuba was issued on 13 April 1922. They planned to stay awhile and then go on to the United States to build a new life. When they left Jamaica, Dora was barely out of her teens. When I was the same age, setting up home in another country had not really crossed my mind — even when the racists said to "go back to where you came from". But Dora did it, so she definitely counts as hero material.

Although Cuba is only ninety miles away from Jamaica, there is a mental as well as physical journey to be made from the hilly contours of Colonels Ridge in the parish of Clarendon to Kingston Harbour and then, by boat, to Cuba. To consider what made them leave, we need to look at what Jamaica was like in the 1920s.

In Dora's time, it was a world of pounds, shillings and pence, British history and a notion of Britain as the

---

2 Hurricane Gilbert was a category 3, 125mph storm. It travelled the length of the island, leaving forty-nine dead, and devastation in its wake. https://jamaica-gleaner.com/article/art-leisure/20200914/when-wild-gilbert-hit-jamaica

"mother country". Jamaica was populated by a white plantocracy and Black "British subjects". Colonels Ridge is a world away from the Jamaican tourist spots you see in the brochures or online. It is a rural area, roughly fifty miles from the capital, Kingston. If you keep on walking up the hill, past the house that Dora grew up in and lived in, traces of the sugar factory are buried deep in the ground on Dawkins Land.[3]

Jamaica was a place where white colonists went to make their fortune. Technically, slavery ended there in 1834 with great resistance from plantation owners, but Britain had its foot on its neck for many years to come. While the slave owners were handsomely compensated for their loss of property, former slaves got nothing, and were forced into scratching a living alongside indentured workers from India and China. The colonisers left in place systems and structures that kept people in their place according to skin colour.[4]

Poverty was entrenched, with high infant mortality rates;

---

3 Henry Dawkins was a major plantation owner in Jamaica (Hall, 2014, p. 31). UCL legacies of British Slave ownership shows that John Williams acted as attorney for the Dawkins family in Colonels Ridge: https://www.ucl.ac.uk/lbs/person/view/2146635749. Compensation awarded for eight slaves in 1836, and two in 1835: https://www.ucl.ac.uk/lbs/estate/view/6366
4 Catherine Hall. "Gendering Property, Racing Capital", *History Workshop Journal*, 78(1), 2014, pp. 22–38. Doi: 10.1093/hwj/dbu024.

there was much sickness and hunger.[5] There was very little work, and what was available was hard, dirty and backbreaking. Working in the cane fields and the sugar factories was the least desirable choice out of very few options. Cuba had the same kind of work on offer, but it was better paid. Travelling to a different country also fed into a desire to be free, to be away from the plantations that had previously owned your body, and to be able to have enough money to buy your own land. Farming your own plot offered a promise of freedom. So, between 1921 and 1922, almost 17,000 people migrated from Jamaica to Cuba.[6] Previous waves of migration saw people going to Panama to build the canal and to Costa Rica to help construct the railroad.[7]

What would life have been like for her in Cuba, for the few years that she lived there? In the early years of the twentieth century, there had been protests by Cubans of African descent against discrimination and Jim Crow-type segregation.[8] Black West Indian "British subjects" were needed but not made welcome. At that time, Cuba was in a state of flux, economically, socially and politically, and although the government wanted to boost the workforce

---

5 Erna Brodber, *The Continent of Black Consciousness: On the History of the African Diaspora from Slavery to the Present Day*. London: New Beacon Books Ltd, 2003.

6 Tracey E. Graham, *Jamaican Migration to Cuba, 1912–1940*. Chicago: University of Chicago, 2012.

7 Ibid.

8 Ibid.

and the population, what they really wanted was white Spanish-speakers.

Dora and Robert must have spent some time in Jatibonico situated in the centre of Cuba, because my mum was born there in 1926. The legacy of slavery and colonialism means that this is all the information I have — I don't know how they lived or what they did while they were there.

What stays with me though, is Dora's kindness. On my first trip, I stayed with her in Colonels Ridge for five weeks. One day, we went to a small market in a nearby town called Kelletts. It was there I witnessed her grace. We had been served our breakfast and I watched as a young man sat down beside her. He didn't say anything, but she must have recognised that he was hungry. She asked for another plate, divided up her food and shared it with him. As he walked away, I realised that she didn't know him.

And then there was the hurricane: Wild Gilbert hit Jamaica on 12 September 1988, when I was about three weeks into my holiday. Dora had gone with the others to collect my mum from the airport when it hit. In the end, there were no flights in or out of the country. It took them three days to get back from Kingston, digging the roads as they went. Thinking about it now, she would have been in her eighties then, but nothing would have stopped her from making that journey. She told me about Hurricane Charlie in 1951 and the devastation that followed.[9] We

---

9 Hurricane Charlie left "154 confirmed dead (including 57 in St. Thomas & 54 in the Corporate area) and 2,000 injured; over 9000 were left homeless". Also, there was extensive damage to shipping and food crops. Several communities were wiped out.

talked about my life in England and to her it sounded like paradise, as I had a job in an office and did not have to do manual labour.

Dora and Robert came back to Jamaica in the late 1920s; her mother had died and they needed to sort out some family business. Dora never left the island again. They had ten children — with an almost fifteen-year span between the first child and the last. Over the years, Dora also took care of many grandchildren and great-grandchildren when their parents left to work overseas.

My inspiration comes from the fact that Dora was born some sixty or so years after emancipation, with the terror of slavery as a living memory, and its consequences as lived experience. Somehow, as a dark-skinned Black woman, she made her place in the world, venturing out from the restrictions of colonial Jamaica in search of a better life. Circumstance brought her "back home", but she made sure that any of her children that wanted to travel did so, and she provided the resources to make it happen.

I wish I'd asked her what Cuba was like in the 1920s, and then I would have fewer gaps and silences in this essay, but what I learned, via those substantial conversations over several years, and seeing the impact of her presence, was to stand firm, to create a sense of who you are, where you are. To gravitate towards freedom, however hard it may be, to liberate yourself through education and knowledge. Equally important, though, is to give back and to dwell

---

See: https://www.nlj.gov.jm/history-notes/History%20of%20 Hurricanes%20and%20Floods%20in%20Jamaica.pdf

in a sense of community. A community that contained multitudes where all life has value.

Dora, I salute you.

AYAKO / CARL NEVILLE

I'm going to talk about my wife, Ayako. I am going to talk about her as the mother of our daughter, Sookie, and by extension the heroism of motherhood itself. You can think of this as a love-letter of a kind, or a public expression of gratitude. A public acknowledgement.

First among the things I want to acknowledge is the sheer labour of giving birth and the level of existential risk that women even in the developed nations enter into in deciding to have a child. I don't believe there is any such equivalent risk, labour or moment of existential uncertainty for men. I don't believe that, outside the most intensive manual jobs or a role in the armed forces or the emergency services, any contemporary employment is as physically or psychologically demanding as childcare. I don't believe that any man will, outside of an accident, face the same degree of physical trauma or experience an equivalent level of pain. No man will have to undergo the anxiety of carrying the child itself or submit to the profound uncertainty of the moment when the contractions start. Nor will they, immediately post-trauma, face the tremendous responsibility for having to care for and nurture the extraordinarily vulnerable form of life that is the new-born.

The heroism I am interested in paying tribute to is not only the quiet, continuous, unshowy daily devotion of motherhood and the enormous reserves of stamina and self-control that it requires, but also the demands of the birth itself and the long process of recovery, the coming to terms with the changes that birth creates physically and psychologically.

I want to acknowledge it because there are few more obvious instances of the combination of bravery and selflessness that defines heroism than that demonstrated by the mother and because in culture more generally it simply isn't acknowledged, except perhaps fleetingly or in unspoken ways. Perhaps without the enforced proximity of work from home, for many families the scale of what is required by childcare might not have been revealed to many men, myself included. Getting out to the office to push a mouse around and deal with irritating clients and customers is light work in comparison.

At one point during the second lockdown in early 2021, a neighbour with a child of two was out in the courtyard at the back of our flats. His daughter was home from daycare with suspected Covid and, in place of having her usual nap, was running around on the grass. "Be nice if she had a little sleep," he said, and our conversation turned to a woman we both saw in the park daily who had a toddler plus twin new-borns. A pause entered into the conversation as we contemplated just how she might be getting through lockdown, with any wider support network she might have had access to closed off to her and a husband out at work. Then our thoughts roamed out to all the families dealing with children with physical or developmental problems, all the single mothers with limited means, all the women in the world with barely enough food for themselves trying to feed and nurture a child, keep it from illness and danger. The enormous toil and toll of fighting not only for your own life but for another's too.

The figure of the hero is most generally male. In some

senses the mother is the opposite of the hero, the long arduous hours of the birth and childcare the mere preconditions for the self-assertion or the display of extraordinary capacities in the face of the wider world that the hero enacts. The hero stands out against the backdrop of mundane life, their aura glitters with a certain Promethean fire, and nothing is more mundane — in its unremittingness, in the drudgery it requires — or more quotidian than producing a child and being its primary caregiver. In some theories of the role of parents in relation to children, it is rejection of the mother that is the foundational act of self-formation, and so mothers must endure this too, to give everything in the knowledge that they are also that which must be rejected.

Yet, in some sense, all the questing and self-surpassing of the male hero, explorer, adventurer, soldier, freedom fighter, plumber of profound depths or scaler of heights founders finally on the monolith that is the mother. Many soldiers, at the end, no matter how brave they have been, are known to cry out for their mothers. They seek, in their hapless floating into the night, the arms of those who guided and comforted them in the enormity of their entering the world as they confront the parallel enormity of their leaving it. You might then say that the rejection of the mother and the motherly and the need for her are the unresolvable and incommensurable tensions that drive us, a perversely productive central aporia.

The model of masculine heroism has, of course, shifted over time from the soldier and explorer to a different figure, that of the entrepreneur — the Atlas, according to some, on whose shoulders the entire world rests. The entrepreneur is valorised as a risk-taker. It is possible to admire the tenacity and vision of the entrepreneur, however, without granting them godlike or more-than-human capacity. They may take risks, but they don't obviously put their lives on the line, only their capital, if it is theirs, a place in the hierarchy, the symbolic order and we could fruitfully contrast the figure of the mother and that of the entrepreneur in asking the question of who supports and sustains the world, upon whose labour it really rests.

That question as to who really carries the world on their backs is answered somewhat differently by the noted paediatrician and psychoanalyst D.W. Winnicott. In a series of lectures on motherhood and the mother-child relationship, in which he coined the phrase "the good-enough mother" and which later became part of a short book, Winnicott explicitly identifies the primal debt that the world owes to mothers. The care that they have provided in their ordinary devotion and their holding of the child, especially in the very early stages of infancy, are the preconditions for a self that is capable of existing more or less peacefully and flexibly in the world. They are the reason we live in a broadly tolerable and shared world, one not overrun with psychopathy and dysfunction. The world exists and endures because we have been mothered. In my own life, during the period when I was most lost and self-destructive, the care that my parents had offered me acted as a floor on how much of myself I was prepared to throw away. There were reserves of their love and hope decanted within me that I felt I had no right to squander. We were too closely entangled in each other for me to damage them too through the damage I was tempted to inflict on myself.

Perhaps by saying mothered I simply mean we have been cared for, been shown love, our existence has been valued and we have learned to value it in some way ourselves.

Perhaps, then, I want to extend my tribute out past the mother I share a child with and out to that mother whose child I am, who talks to me more freely these days, now I am finally on the other side, in the shared realm of parenthood, about my own birth, how she was alone in the hospital, back in the days before fathers routinely attended births, had an epidural and was barely conscious when I passed out into the world and how the doctor who came in to stitch her up was drunk. Perhaps, really, I want to extend it out even further to all those who stand at the thresholds of life and work every day in its dim parentheses, in hospitals, care homes, hospices, and find ways when the symbols have broken down and disorganisation reigns, to mother us, who have found a way to guide us again through the *terra incognita*.

Often those people are women. Perhaps I simply want to express gratitude to them, to the carers, all of whom fulfil in some way the role of the mother for us and who we need deeply, no matter how far we think we might have risen from that need. Perhaps I just want to express gratitude to the women on the much-derided *Mumsnet* who calm the fears and anxieties of other mothers and fathers, my own included, with their own hard-earned experience, to the midwives who sustain and support other women through labour day after day. And, at the other end of that journey, to the woman who met my sister and I at the doorway the night my father died and whose words and demeanour soothed and calmed my terrible fear as, conjuring up my best facsimile of the heroic mode, I strode down into the underworld to see him, all his own heroism spent now, and to hold his hand for the last time.

ELLEN RIPLEY / RYANN DONNELLY

I have been turned on by goo, slime and ooze since before I learned what cum was; since before I could cum. This essay is about my hero, Lieutenant Ellen Ripley.

Within the context of the *Alien* films, Ripley is the hero because she defeats the villains. This essay will explore how this ascendency is conveyed through representations, and achieved through relationships that I will broadly describe as Queer for their position outside heteronormative frameworks of desire and intimacy. I am referring to her subversive adaptations of motherhood, and her violent encounters with other maternal figures that often produce iterations of Queer sexuality. However, the reason I cherish her above any other heroic figure is because her cinematic heroism ultimately relies on her engagement with an absolutely hideous amount of goo.

When I question the source of my attraction to this kind of substance, I locate a logical possibility in seeing two mouths linked for an instant by a thin strand of saliva as they pull away from a kiss; at some point when I was young. An otherwise invisible interior was exposed that appeared to me liquid, warm and live. I found the pace of its movement sensual and wanted to feel it all over my body — in motion, and then submerged within it, and then filled by it. As it pertains to this essay, I also like that a delicate spit thread is formally comparable to the alien in its infancy as shown in the *Alien* prequel, *Prometheus*. Both innocuous beginnings forecast heaving, wet monstrosities. My interest in goo later developed alongside my encounters with its varietals in sexual contexts, sure. I have enjoyed cum, sweat, tears, mucus and spit being revealed to me through the consensual manipulation of the nerves and tissues that are typically expected to dam bodily fluids. Goo did become representative of connection and trust, but in terms of its erotic capacity, it didn't need to be exchanged. It was really always enough on its own. I do not find goo erotic because it is cum-like. I find cum erotic because it is goo. I'll now draw on a few key scenes to illustrate my affections for Ripley, the film, and all its sticky stuff.

Directed by Ridley Scott in 1979, the first *Alien* film sees members of a commercial spaceship, the *Nostromo*, taken off course by their malevolent computer system, MU-TH-UR (Mother). This is the first of several examples across the film series where classical stereotypes of mothers as caring and nurturing are defied. As a computer, Mother also offers a model of motherhood that refuses to be defined in biological terms, and does not comport with classical models of family. This suggests that your "mother" might not have given birth to you; she might not even have a body. And as the film will show, just because your mother made you, or informed you, or constructed you, doesn't mean she can't be rotten.

Mother re-routes the crew in order to investigate the source of what may be a distress signal, "under penalty of total forfeiture of shares" — i.e., the crew won't be paid if they don't do what she says. It is later revealed that the crew has been misled by Mother. The true purpose of their mission is to recover an alien life form whose "perfection" — according to the sociopathic android who colludes with Mother and allows the alien to enter the ship against Ripley's orders — is defined by its "hostility… unclouded by conscience, remorse, or delusions of morality", so that it may be used by the weapons division of the company that employs the crew members of the *Nostromo*.

Throughout the film, the crew refer to the company exclusively as "The Company". The anonymity suggests this could be any/every company — or capitalism generally — and emphasises an ominous detachment necessary to The Company prioritising the monetisation of the alien's capacity for sweeping death over the lives of those in service to it. The Company's motives come to light after the alien murders several members of the crew. Ripley seeks answers about the mission from Mother, who confirms that her "Priority one" is to "insure return of the organism for analysis… crew expendable". Mother is exposed as violent and deceitful after accommodating the demands of The Company instead of refusing to jeopardize the lives of the crew, all of whom have relied on her for information and guidance.

I do recognise that Mother is not making these decisions autonomously. Mother *is* The Company; she enacts its will. This offers another view of motherhood that is alternative in its fragmentation and status as shared or cooperative. Moreover, this motherhood is shared with an entity that is not identified as Father or positioned as having any necessary romantic link to Mother. Mother's betrayal of the crew's innate trust further reinforces this departure from maternal norms. This is followed by the broader destruction of the family model when Ripley destroys Mother after escaping from her on a smaller shuttle craft, and eventually defeating the alien that has also snuck on board. But, significant aspects of *Alien*'s premise are reprised in the 1986 sequel, *Aliens*, directed by James Cameron.

In *Aliens*, The Company sends Ripley back to the planet LV-426 where the alien was first encountered. She is meant to act as an advisor to the marine corps, ostensibly in hopes of recovering a group of colonists with whom communication has been unexpectedly lost. Predictably though, the project of recovering the alien for nefarious corporate ends re-enters the narrative as the underlying motive for the mission.

When Ripley arrives, she discovers a child who is the only survivor of the group. Clearly traumatised, the child is wide-eyed, covered in filth, with wild and matted hair. The relationship that develops between the child and Ripley is key to exploring alternative models of the maternal. But, given the common appraisal of motherhood as an extension of womanhood, the ways in which gender identity is subverted are a crucial aspect of this project to consider.

Ripley learns the child's name from a photo marked, "Second Grade Citizen Award: Rebecca Jorden". "Rebecca" appears healthier, happier (she smiles), is more kempt and femme: her hair is brushed, smooth and blonde, and she wears a prim, collared dress. But, when Ripley calls the child by this name, she is corrected. The child tells Ripley to use the name "Newt", which rejects the feminine connotations of the name "Rebecca" and of the image of Rebecca.

By adopting the name of a creature rather than a conventional name for a person, moreover, there is a fundamental rejection of the binary system of gender that organises the human. She is neither masculine nor feminine — she is, more broadly, animal. This effect is further reinforced as intentional, given that newts are amphibians able to change their sex in response to extreme environments. The name troubles notions of gender in ways that are consistent with later subversions of gender that, importantly, rely on Ripley's relationship *with* Newt. To establish Newt's non-binary, anti-human identity aligns Newt with Ripley's subversion of the gendered role of Mother; and avoids Newt being positioned as a tool in the execution of that project. As soon as Ripley encounters Newt, she guards and protects the character; and later makes a commitment to maintain this care. Ripley says, "I'm not going to leave you, Newt. I mean that. That's a promise... I cross my heart... and hope to die". Ripley's adoption of Newt defies notions of motherhood as a biologically determined role in the same way that the figure of Mother did in *Alien*. However, Ripley does offer the care and protection that Mother did not; again, troubling the consistency with which maternal care is enacted, or what it is expected to involve. Motherhood is positioned as an elected role.

Threats to the biological determination of maternal identity are further explored in how motherhood is achieved by the Queen Alien — the mother of all other aliens. In *Alien Resurrection*, it is established that the Queen is parthenogenic. Though much of this essay has sought to confront notions of what constitutes maternal behaviour, and to challenge maternal care as a "natural" or innate quality of womanhood, or an effect of biological motherhood, acknowledging that parthenogenesis is a natural process also helps re-think the very standards of "natural" reproduction. That is, "natural reproduction" is not always heterosexual. Parthenogenesis is displayed in some invertebrates such as aphids; it is asexual reproduction. As a parthenogenic organism, the Queen is able to reproduce without fertilization of her ovum, and — like Ripley and Mother — is a mother that neither has nor requires a mate. I have established that Mother, Ripley, and the Queen confront classical models of motherhood — and by extension womanhood — through their behaviour, their subversion of biologically determined identity, their lack of sexual or romantic partnerships and their methods of reproduction that refuse heterosexual copulation. Having explored the effect of Ripley's violent encounter with Mother, I would now like to explore the implications of Ripley's conflicts with the Queen.

In the final scene of *Aliens*, Ripley descends into the moist tangles of the alien nest with a grenade launcher to recover Newt, who has been abducted. Newt is bound in a clear, massive, viscous web. To create this, and the other varieties of shiny, milky, globular and gelatinous surfaces and fluids seen throughout the film, the prop department used materials such as K-Y Jelly, eggs, oysters and lamb intestines. Ripley frees Newt and runs with her child against her chest, but halts when she arrives at hundreds of oozing alien pods. The ovipositor of the Queen releases another slimy egg, which remains tethered by strands of thick, clinging discharge as she slowly stretches away. Within the slick, veiny, tubular anatomy of the Queen are hundreds of eggs, pulsing and squirming. The Queen slowly articulates her insect-like limbs, opens her series of mouths and bares her long, needle-like teeth to Ripley, whose destruction of her alien children has made Ripley the target of the Queen's wrath. Ripley fires her flamethrower into the distance to establish unexpected conditions of the encounter: let us leave, and I won't destroy your babies. Ripley and Newt slowly back out of the nest, but Ripley torches the eggs and fires into the Queen's body, which creates explosive splashes of mucous, puss and slime.

This violence between Ripley and the Queen is motivated by their shared desire to protect their children, which re-frames motherhood as violent. This violence is rendered sexual and offers iterations of queer intimacies (different ways of fucking and cumming) as informed by my appraisal of the sexual qualities of goo. Importantly, goo is not blood. It does not typically signal violence or injury, despite its proximity to blood as something forced from one's interior. Its release is more commonly negotiated through pleasure. In this regard, the prevalence of goo, and the frequent replacement of blood by goo in *Alien* and *Aliens*, refuses conventional ways of making violence legible, instead conflating the violent with the sexual through the aesthetics of cum. In this way, the conflict between Ripley and the Queen can be read as a homoerotic sadism, where the homogenous quality of their eroticism is not defined by their shared womanhood but by their shared status as mothers. To protect their young, and effectively their roles as mothers, they get pleasure from harming the mother whose young will threaten their own, and the visual coding of this violence renders this erotic.

These conflicts and erotic coding also inform a way of reading the Queen's reproduction as another site of Queer intimacy. Given that continuing to produce or actively mother the aliens will result in continued attacks on the Queen by Ripley, we might qualify this act as a kind of masochism. The Queen gets pleasure from the act of reproduction, despite this being the source of the pain that will be inflicted upon her by Ripley. Considering the parthenogenic status of her reproduction, moreover, we might also see this as autoerotic. Both readings rely on violence being delivered by dripping, slippery bodies, or the enacted violence by Ripley, which makes another body wet, dripping and wounded.

In her conflicts with Mother and the Queen, Ripley directs the expletive "YOU BITCH!" at both of these characters (and only these characters). This marks a shared antagonism directed at Ripley by these characters that leads to conflicts which explore fortified deviations from historical narratives of motherhood, womanhood, and sexuality or sexual pleasure. I do not think I could see it this way were I less enamoured with goo.

WILE E. COYOTE /MAT OSMAN

© *Credit: Warner Bros/TCD/Prod.DB/Alamy*

1976. The year of the Pistols, Nadia Comaneci and Travis Bickle. Heroes to many, but not for me yet, obviously, at just nine years old. Instead, I'm raptly prone on our living-room floor with my breakfast in front of me — Ready Brek in winter, Weetabix in the summer — and the room is hot with that baked ozone smell of a Seventies' TV warming up. Breakfast time means cartoons; more specifically it means those *Looney Toons* shorts that pepper the more educational programmes with a dash of anarchy in the same way that cigarettes would come to punctuate the working day once I was older. I am lying there waiting for one character in particular. I didn't care much for Bugs Bunny — even at that age I could spot a bully. Pepé Le Pew was creepy (a borderline sex-pest) and Porky Pig was too much of a nerd even for a boy who had books full of self-designed Crystal

Palace kits. But one animated hero did shine through — the true star of the Looney Tooniverse.

He's called Road-Runnerus Digestus in *Zipping Along*, and Hungrii Flea-Bagius in *Beep Prepared*. Calling him Overconfidentii Vulgaris in *Zoom at the Top* prepares you for the catastrophic hubris to come (and being dubbed Caninus Nervous Rex in *War and Pieces* gives you an idea of his fragile mental state).

Wile E. Coyote. The name has always bugged me, actually. It's not Daff E. Duck or Tweet E. Pie, so what would have been wrong with a simple Wily Coyote? (Though the dictionary does tell me that Wile is indeed a name. It means "occupational surname for a trapper", which would be perfect if Wile E. actually ever succeeded in truly trapping anything.)

Even compared with my primary school pupil existence, Wile E.'s life was rigid, almost aesthetic in its simplicity. He rose from some forever unseen bed, unpacked whichever complex contraption was going to help him in his pursuit of the Roadrunner, and left to do deadly battle with his nemesis across the arid badlands of the southwestern desert. The word "battle" is misleading, really, because it implies some kind of parity. He chased and harried, he lay in wait and he schemed. But no matter how many bombs he disguised as bird seed, how many enormous magnets he employed, every plan ended fruitlessly, with the Roadrunner unscathed and the coyote broken in various violent and demoralising ways. Barely a day went by that he wasn't somehow burnt to a blackened cinder or shattered into so many tiny pieces that he had to be swept up in a dustpan and brush. The whole process was as brutally formulaic as most of my favourite art of the time — the Famous Five,

Showaddywaddy — but it had the added frisson of that most adult of concepts: failure.

On into my twenties, and I watched the coyote still. He became perfect stoned watching. The jokes were so clearly telegraphed that I was helpless with laughter even before the denouement. Wile E. hoisting an anvil high overhead, his knife out to cut the rope? Wile E. snuggling down into his ACME cannon, fuse fizzing? Well, nuff said. Around this time, I saw both my first actual coyote (majestic, but with, even from a tour-bus window, an undeniable sense of melancholy) *and* my first roadrunner (beyond drab, like some ADHD-raddled song-thrush).

In my fifties, although I still love the cartoons, I find them harder to watch. Now that I'm old enough to have seen friends fuck up their lives irredeemably, watching someone fail repeatedly — indeed, fail repeatedly trying the same thing over and over again — is less amusing. Wile E.'s desperate search for fulfilment is now tinged with a kind of existential despair. But still, there's a nobility to his quest, a quixotic tilting at windmills, that keeps me rooting for him.

What have I learned from four decades of watching a cartoon coyote fruitlessly pursue a cartoon bird? What lessons are encoded in those eight-minute vignettes of violence?

Firstly, I learned early that a certain class of people (or flightless birds) will be able to ignore universal, set rules, later on in life. These roadrunner people will stroll, blithely, through train tunnels that, immediately upon *your* reaching them, will turn back into unforgiving rock. Magnets don't affect them; fire cannot touch them. Gravity itself will look the other way; when life's road drops away beneath our feet (and it will, oh, it will) *they'll* walk on air without a care while we spiral, noiselessly to the canyon floor (followed inevitably by the very ledge on which we both once stood).

A second lesson: knowing where you have gone wrong in life is no guarantee that you will come up with an alternative strategy. Another hero of mine, Peter Cook, who resembles Wile E. insomuch as he never achieved what others expected of him but gave millions pleasure while not achieving it, once said: "I have learned from my mistakes, and I am sure I could repeat them exactly". If Wile E. Coyote were to hear those words then I imagine he would hoist up one of his trademark signs with "Amen, brother" written across it.

Thirdly: Hope is better than expectation. Wile E.'s pursuit of the Roadrunner is the cartoon equivalent of gig-work — repetitive, poorly recompensed and dangerous — but he never loses his hope, or more importantly his élan. We are all of us faced with the grind of daily chores, from the office to the dishwasher to the garage, but few of us have the grace to go about them with the sheer gusto of Wile E. strapping on his thousandth pair of mechanised wooden wings.

Fourthly: Technology that's supposed to make your life easier will in fact forever fuck up, spectacularly, and it'll be you that has to clear up the mess. Big corporations aren't your friends; once they have your money, they'll wash their hands of you. (Though in fact Wile E. Coyote would have made a wonderful tech bro. "Move fast and break things," "Whatever doesn't kill you makes you stronger," "Fail fast, fail often": these are his kind of mottos.)

Fifthly (and most importantly of all): Never, *ever*, tie yourself to a tree, then bend it over, taut, to fashion a makeshift catapult. You *will* be slammed back and forth repeatedly into the earth, over and over, until you walk away shaped like a concertina, playing a wheezy tune the whole way.

I suppose there are some Roadrunner-hearted people reading this, people who resemble that avian avatar of privilege in that the world will forever rearrange itself around them, who will never be aware of how their advantages have greased life's wheels for them. But for the rest of us, well it's just another morning. It's time to strap on our over-sized roller-skates and cardboard wings. Time to scatter those ACME-brand ball-bearings across the road, light the touchpaper on the gargantuan rockets strapped to our backs, and aim ourselves down the road. It's a new day. Happy hunting, folks.

Photo by Karim Benammar

ALPHONSO LINGIS & BRUNO LATOUR / GRAHAM HARMAN

By the spring of 1990, I was just months away from a Bachelor's Degree. Philosophy had been my passion for six years, whether through individual reading in high school or the classically-oriented curriculum at St. John's College. Heidegger was not on the St. John's reading list at that point, but I tore through his works in private; even so, at that point I had little direct exposure to more recent authors in philosophy. It was the end of March when a generous friend lent me his car, and I made the roughly three-hour drive from Annapolis to Penn State University, keen to visit the campus and town before accepting their offer of graduate admission. Without knowing it, I was about to encounter the dominant influence of my postgraduate studies.

Alphonso Lingis would have been fifty-six years old at the time, just a few years older than I am now. Some American campus chieftains gain that reputation through task-masterish discipline and stinting praise to desperate students who duel each other for the master's recognition. Lingis at Penn State was a completely different sort of phenomenon: an anti-hierarchical shaman who greeted each new visitor as if they were potentially the world's most interesting person. His house itself was legendary: an odd edifice placed directly in the middle of a block, haunting rather than haunted, with the entry gate accessible only from an alley. In certain currents of the Penn State community, the Lingis household was the most treasured destination in the town of State College. Early in my stay, a graduate student took me for a night-time visit that is forever seared into memory. There were the expected thousands of books, many of them in French, but with unusual section labels arranging them into such categories as "balderdash" and "rubbish". A tribal spear from God-knows-what-country stood near the front door, with Lingis frequently joking that it was reserved for his most unpleasant department colleague should he ever return; he had come years earlier on an evil academic errand and was summarily ejected. Tropical birds were visible throughout the front room, and Lingis was feeding fruit salad to his pet toucans at the precise moment of my arrival. While doing so, he openly mused about missing the octopus that used to dwell in his aquarium and was discussing his plans to obtain a new one. Lingis would later construct a shark tank in his basement, years after I had left town. But his celebrated bathroom, mirrored on every surface including the floor, was already home to the beehive that many will remember. And the guest bedroom was already decorated with an impressive collection of multi-coloured beetles pinned to the wall. Although a conservative St. John's faculty member had warned in advance that Lingis was "a Pied Piper who preys on student resentment of authority", this had only increased my excitement in meeting him, and this first encounter was enough to know that this was the teacher for me. My interest was Heidegger, and Lingis was a specialist in French thought, but I could hardly have cared less about this discrepancy.

But while the eccentric personality of Alphonso Lingis has delighted generations of friends and observers, I was more influenced by his rock-solid diligence and his systematic thoughts across numerous themes, perhaps a surprise to those critics who find his books too episodic. Though some of my undergraduate teachers had published a book or two, it was bracing that first night to hear Lingis discuss a wide spectrum of publishing projects he had underway. Soon I would discover the excellence of his prose style, which may have no equal in his generation of Americans. And the Lingis who welcomed spontaneous midnight visitors to his home too often overshadows the Lingis I knew, who was graced with an almost astonishing work ethic. As a starving graduate student, I was sometimes allowed to stay in his conference hotel rooms free of charge. No matter how early I awakened, Lingis would already be at work on his nearly silent portable typewriter, pursuing his longstanding habit of doing his writing early in the morning. The rest of the day was for conversation and the pursuit of offbeat experience.

A semester with Lingis ran roughly as follows. A course would feature recent rather than classical authors — in my first semester it was Baudrillard, Serres and Deleuze/ Guattari — and Lingis would spend half of each class reading an invariably beautiful essay loosely related to that night's assigned pages. Then came a moderately long break, followed by freewheeling discussion in which students did most of the talking. The audience was not restricted to Penn State graduate students, but often featured bohemians and fringe intellectuals from town, along with motorcyclists or weightlifters known to Lingis personally. Term papers were due on the final night of the semester. Lingis would then file an automatic grade of A for everyone in the class and depart the next day for his favoured travel site of the time. Although in the 1960s he was often in Paris, by 1990 he was generally either in Rio de Janeiro, Bangkok or Manila whenever the need arose to track him down. After a delay of two or three weeks, each of his students would receive a typed letter in the mail from one of these far-flung locations, containing sensitive and detailed commentary on whatever it was we had written: sometimes critical, but always deeply encouraging. My work for the Master's Degree was sent to Lingis *poste restante* in Guatemala City, and though I hardly believed it would reach him, his comments in return — from Brazil, I believe — changed the course of my intellectual career. In those early days I was still in thrall to a holistic reading of Heidegger's tool-analysis, using the Levinasian notion of sensual enjoyment as a counterweight. Although the comments from Lingis were largely reassuring, he openly expressed doubt as to whether anything like a unified tool-system could possibly exist. This planted a seed of doubt that grew, a year later, into my first crude formulation of object-oriented ontology.

We turn now to 1998: not even a decade later in calendar time, but almost a different lifetime in the career of a young thinker. A lot can happen to us between the ages of twenty-two and thirty. By the late 1990s I had still published nothing but was known among fellow students as the author of charismatic papers and a developing philosophical position. Since relations with my doctoral advisor were relatively hostile, I felt almost totally isolated and in a generally precarious position. Although my topic (Heidegger) is widely known for his grave and pompous authorial tone, I had never enjoyed that aspect of his work, and was already presenting his ideas in the somewhat irreverent way that my readers know. While entering the final stage of dissertation work, it was suggested by chance that I read Bruno Latour, and *We Have Never Been Modern* was recommended as the best place to start. Although it would be untrue to say I was hooked on Latour from the first paragraph, it took twenty or thirty pages at most to realise that his work was exactly what I needed as an antidote to Heidegger. Latour was witty, contemporary, lucid and full of admiration for artificial objects where Heidegger could only express backwaterish disdain. Within months I had read many or most of his books, and a professor I liked had asked me to make a presentation on Latour to the university community. He attended that lecture, and strongly advised that I send it to Latour himself, remarking that famous thinkers have fewer positive interactions than one might expect, adding that he had similar luck as a graduate student making contact with such philosophers as Derrida and Davidson.

In two weeks at most, I received a message from Latour that could not have been warmer. This ended in an instant most of the sufferings of my student career. No longer would I worry about the feedback of this or that advisor or evaluation committee; if I was able to write things of interest to a world-class intellectual, the path ahead was cleared of the previous institutional obstacles. In some ways we were opposites: Latour a famous thinker and I an obscure fresh PhD; Latour a despiser of Heidegger and I an ardent fan; Latour a declared pragmatist in outlook and I a philosophical realist who felt that pragmatist authors were empty calories. Still, we somehow clicked, even if relative youth made me more often the helper and listener. This good chemistry continued, with sporadic rough patches, once we met in London the following year. Despite being nearly a generation younger, Latour was a classic *paterfamilias* figure in a manner utterly foreign to Lingis, who was more of a rebellious older brother. Eventually I learned that Latour and his wife Chantal were born in precisely the same years as my own father and mother, which emphasised further the difference in age and stature.

Before long I became one of those who would comment on his drafts, provide feedback on his latest ideas and occasionally house-sit his Latin Quarter flat when Bruno and Chantal were away at their summer home in Châtelperron. I was able to invite him to Cairo as a visiting speaker in my early years in Egypt, and there the intellectual relationship further deepened. Although in some ways quintessentially French, Latour has always been most at home in the world of the Anglophone social sciences, with its detailed footnotes and fondness for teamwork. This sort of intellectual lifestyle drew dozens, even hundreds of people into his personal network, and he was always finding new ways to bring them into communication, with himself and each other. Although he sometimes claimed (sincerely, but inaccurately) that his work was completely ignored, Latour's circle of supportive colleagues is vast, and to know him is to meet interesting people almost constantly. It happened that we reached an intellectual impasse early on, since Latour's actor-network theory completely precludes my own commitment to real and inaccessible entities. For the most part these debates were enjoyable, though I do recall a handful of explosive and painful quarrels. When I finally began to publish my own work, Latour was no less supportive of me than of other young people in his circle. There was some push-and-pull in which he supported my publications with occasional reservations. Whatever the details of our disagreements, nothing is more helpful for a young person than to be taken seriously by someone who has already arrived at the top. For that I will always be grateful, and Bruno Latour remains on my personal shortlist of heroes.

Yet my gratitude to Latour goes well beyond the personal sphere. Although he is still widely regarded as more of an anthropologist and sociologist of science than a philosopher, and though neither the analytic nor continental camps of philosophy have realised his importance, to associate with Latour in the years when I knew him best was to witness intellectual history in the making. Philosophy today comes mostly in one of two flavours: the first is a science-worshipping naturalism that does little to account for complex social and technical artifacts, and the second is a lukewarm transcendental approach that restricts itself to the relation between thought and world. Latour blows this modern schema apart by destroying the assumption that reality consists of precisely two domains — the natural and the cultural — and by treating all of them equally as actors. Whenever I feel the need to regain a clear sense of where modern philosophy comes up short, it is always Latour's works to which I return. Getting to know his work saved me, and not just me, decades of wasted time. Like every career that yields an irreversible breakthrough, his has both the air and substance of the heroic.

PAULA REGO / CHRISTIANA SPENS

I had been living in Glasgow for about six months when I went to see the Paula Rego exhibition over in Edinburgh, titled *Obedience and Defiance*. I was reviewing it for a magazine, and taking the chance to see two friends, Sam and Miranda, at the same time. I'd met them through other friends during the Fringe Festival that summer, and they had recently moved in together.

It was November now, and I had also just started seeing someone new, following a long period of personal turmoil. I had become a mother and a divorcee in the space of a few years; I had lost my father. I had been torturing myself with the ghosts of boyfriends past — and friends, and my dad, and any other demon who would take up the invitation to play havoc with my head.

Rego's work had always drawn me in, though I had never seen any of it in the flesh. I remembered the first works I had come across, though — a series of illustrations of dark fairy tales, when I was a teenager — and since then I had returned to her work routinely with a sense of uncanny comfort. She spoke — or drew — in a language I recognised innately and primally. She wove fables and religion and bodies and sexuality all together, creating these oppressive, heroic, somehow liberating scenes.

I was in a fog the day I took the train over to Edinburgh, as I was most days then, and despite many coffees was no less dazed when I met Sam and Miranda in the museum. We hugged and walked into the first room, catching up as we looked at her early work. We had only been standing there for about three minutes, however, when an irate man interrupted us, eyes bulging. "Excuse me!" he bellowed, a few inches from my face. "Will you please stop talking! I am TRYING to HEAR the PAINTINGS!" Sam burst out laughing, and then quickly corrected himself. "Oh," he said. "You're not joking." No, he was not! His aggression was entirely intentional. A middle-aged man loudly trying to silence us. I tried to contain my fury, turning to laughter with Sam and Miranda instead, as we left. But really! Here was an entire exhibition about hitting back against the oppressive moods and egos of men, and it was playing out right in front of us. It felt like a sort of sacrilege that he was even here. But also a joke.

We went upstairs, anyway, to find Rego's *Dog Woman* series — works produced over the course of her career, from the drawing *Dog Woman* (1952), made the year Rego entered the Slade School of Art, and met her partner, painter Vic Willing, to *Sleeper* (1994), one of her first pastel works, in which a woman lies on her master's jacket like a sleeping dog. Throughout these works, which marked not only different stages in her career, but also in her life and particularly her turbulent, complex relationship with her husband, the central themes of obedience and defiance were clear and vindicating. They gave me fire, lit me up, elevated something within.

Having grown up under the strict and oppressive fascist regime of António de Oliveira Salazar in Portugal, I wrote down in my notes, *in which the state and the Catholic Church worked complicitly to control their subjects (especially women), Rego's work consistently and defiantly addressed complex power dynamics in various intersecting areas, whether through the prism of personal, romantic relationships or through overtly political issues such as war and political exile. In her* Dog Woman *series, she used the image and mannerisms of dogs to explore the nuances and complexities of these power dynamics.*

Sometimes a master, sometimes the obedient dog-like creature, Rego's characters equated female and male sexualities and other behaviours to the characteristics of dogs, and in their associations with one another, and other overt motifs from political discourse and Portuguese folklore, she connected these seemingly distinct issues. Was the master her husband or the Church? The king or her mother? Her own sexuality? Her characters, regardless of their roles, dominated us all with the same compelling combination of defiance and submission to their roles, their physical (often constrained) form, their closed and confusing environments.

We walked around some more, taking in the domineering submissives and constrained masters. In *Snare* (1987), a girl in a voluminous mauve dress loomed over a dog, mocking its powerlessness and impotence. In *Untitled* (1986), another young girl, wearing a hairband, put a chain around the dog's neck. Later on, women themselves resembled dogs: in *Sleeper* (1994), an adult woman laid in a doglike pose; it was not clear whether she has been punished or whether she takes comfort in nuzzling with her master's jacket — or indeed, both. In *Lush* (1994), another woman sat openly like a dog, moody and yet unapologetic. In the *Abortion Triptych* (1998), women stoically endured illegal abortions out of social and financial necessity. In *The Crime of Father Amaro* series, a young girl is caught up in an illegal affair with a priest.

I sat down and read more about Rego's life. She had met

Vic at the Slade when she was nineteen, and he was already married. She went on to terminate several pregnancies as a student before going back to Portugal to have their daughter. They later married, after he left his wife and they reunited, and had two more children. He then developed multiple sclerosis and Rego became his carer in the later years of his life. Their roles therefore evolved in complex, difficult ways: Rego was a young lover, a "fallen woman", a mother, a wife, a carer. Perhaps because I had just started seeing a new boyfriend and fallen in love completely and fast, reading about Rego's complicated life felt especially prescient, and much needed. She understood the messiness of life and love, of power and submission, obedience and defiance.

Life necessitated stark changes in role, I knew well — far more complex than notions of "master" and "dog" would at first glance explain. Her paintings revealed precisely this: how binaries of power dynamics were simply markers that signalled vast depths of human emotion, as we struggled to love and endure one another in wider systems of oppression.

I thought of them all, then — the ghosts and demons, the men in my life. How we struggled to love and endure one another, on whatever level. And then I couldn't help but forgive, though I had not been trying to. I never really intended to, wasn't sure I ever really understood the point of forgiveness. But I couldn't hold it all against them anymore. They were people in paintings, creatures, twisted and dark and sublime. I'd shared their shadows long enough to know that much.

Though she sought to be a painter, "like a man" — an "art monster" — Rego could never escape being a woman, just as her subjects could not (and perhaps would not) escape being dogs, I wrote. *Their passion is wrought from sacrifice. In* Sit *(1994), a pregnant woman crosses her feet, and in so doing mimics, subtly, the Crucifixion. In the series of etchings exposing the horror of female genital mutilation, Rego's victims recall tortured saints, despite the brevity and minimalism of their production. Using these familiar motifs from religious paintings, she elevates the everyday suffering of women, recognising it and confronting it head-on, never losing the nuance, ambiguity and darkness implicit in these scenes and situations.*

Rego saw the similarities between art practice and romantic relationships. "Painting is erotic," she said, "you do it with your hand. It's the same feeling of being possessed by desire." In painting, as in eroticism, she was defiant, even as she was consumed. All of her characters were defiant and consumed in their situation. All of her artworks were defiant and consuming. They depicted suffering, oppression and cruelty and yet her figures consistently embraced it.

There was a film showing downstairs in the gallery, and we sat down to watch it. It had been made by her son and also featured her daughter, who said of her mother that endurance of pain became a sort of proof of love. "Look how much I will bear for you," her paintings seemed to say — and not simply to her late husband, but to life itself, and to God, despite the Church. "Look how much I must love you, to endure all this." I thought of my new love, how he was everything, already — how quickly I felt entirely consumed by love. But in this life? It felt so fragile, and so perfect. I nuzzled into my master's jacket, waiting for his return.

The film also talked about how Rego had suffered from prolonged periods of depression, and how in those times she "drew herself out of it". She "gave fear a face", and in so doing she mastered it. In these images of suffering, confused desire, love and pain, Rego mastered, in a sense, these forces (and people) in the act of painting or drawing itself. She endured and expressed aggression; she was the master and the dog — to painting, to desire, to the political environments she finds herself in, often viscerally.

I walked around some more, leaving Miranda and Sam by smaller paintings, and came across *Angel* (1998), part of *The Crime of Father Amaro* series, in which Rego depicted a woman in a silk dress, in gold and silver, holding the symbols of a sword and a sponge, her hair pulled back in a dark bun. She was entirely defiant, her expression serious and yet somehow teasing, baiting. Was she asking for confrontation? Was she asking to sacrifice herself? Was she asking, after all this, for more? This was heroism, to me. This was my heroine. *The Avenging Angel.* Rego.

The man downstairs was not the last to take issue with us. Another paced around, then told Miranda off for taking a photo of an etching. More huffed and storm out. The men were triggered, apparently; there was a funny feeling in the air. We smiled to one another, rolled our eyes, looked the men in the eye when they complained to us, did not move. Surely Rego would enjoy this: how quickly her audience mimicked her own work, how we all submitted to her art, one way or another. How we became disciples of Rego.

Later on, back in my flat, my son asleep, I went back to her work, flicking through the exhibition catalogue. Over and over again, these strong, stubborn faces, and the unconditional loyalty and love that they expressed. The purest, most visceral religion, she offered here. I could only bow to that. I wanted her religion, her heroism. To be mastered by it, freed by it. I only wanted that.

I took out my pencils and paper and kept drawing, as the months went on. I drew dark shadowy monsters, I drew friends. I drew strangers in bars, men who played on my mind. I drew the one I loved. I drew my own shadows, entangled with theirs. I drew my son. I kept drawing until I was peaceful again, like I was praying. I prayed to Paula Rego's *Avenging Angel*: *please watch over me, please see me, as I see you.* She cut through my fear with her sword, cleansed me of that endemic shame. I slept, relaxed. I drew myself back into life, having been erased.

In Rego's work, I had found the perfect articulation of a sense that existence and personal identity is inherently interconnected, precarious, messy, and yet loving. To be victorious amid this means becoming resilient enough to exist through an ever-changing sense of embodiment and disembodiment, where other people and events may take and dominate and disappear and turn away. It is to understand that loss — of other people and even, at times, ourselves — is part of living. We are more fluid than we admit, and so, too, more connected to everyone else.

And so, I found a way to reconcile myself to this flux. By drawing and writing, I could reappear, be visible to myself again. I found a way to articulate and visualise the pain of losing others, and how I existed with and through them, as they did through me. Art became not a solace as such, but a way to exist and emerge, a part of living, a form of strength. Drawing, and heroism, for me, was personified in Paula Rego's *Avenging Angel* — a spiritual calling, a ritual as everyday and necessary as cooking and sleeping and waking, a way of life.

Photo by José Jordan.

JOSEP ALMUDÉVER MATEU / MARCUS BARNETT

With the passing of Josep Almudéver Mateu in May 2021, the world lost its last International Brigader. The news struck me peculiarly: it only occurred to me there and then that I'd never considered a world inhabited by no *brigadistas*. Despite only becoming politically engaged as a teenager nearly seventy years after the beginning of the Spanish Civil War, it was easy to spot those remaining of the 59,000 people who offered their lives in defence of democracy. In the pensioners' movement, my nana could count the nonagenarian Jack Jones — who was wounded badly in Spain — as a nationally leading comrade until his death in 2009. They could be found at rallies against war and privatisation across the country, exceptionally old and exceptionally spritely, fighting on. To paraphrase Abe Osheroff, one of the last surviving American volunteers, their ships were sinking but their cannons kept firing.

Josep was born in Marseille in 1919. His father, Vicente, was a committed rebel. When a local priest in his Valencian village of Alcàsser forced the cancellation of a local dance, Almudéver senior attempted to burn his church down in retaliation. As a way to escape the Spanish authorities, he fled to Marseilles. It was there he met his wife, a circus worker also hailing from Valencia, and they soon had three children. Following a brief stint in Morocco, the family returned to Alcàsser, where the realities of Spain's semi-feudal system were clear. The vast majority of villagers were peasants, of whom 60% were illiterate. A single landowner owned more than 10% of the land, and Josep would later recall with bitterness how the village's men would be forced to stand in the local square at sunrise every morning, where they were chosen or rejected by the landowner's lackeys for daily work.

It should come as no surprise that Josep regarded 14 April 1931 — the declaration of the Spanish Republic — as an "event of incredible happiness". King Alfonso XIII had been deposed, and a new constitution enshrined women's suffrage, legalised divorce and protected freedom of speech while tackling the institutional privileges of the Catholic Church and the monarchy. In an interview recently republished in *Tribune*, Josep told Denis Rogatyuk about the "first euphoric week" of the Republic and the "explosion of freedom in the streets", where peasants and workers demonstrated in huge numbers, holding aloft banners and pictures of leading radicals and revolutionary martyrs.

From early childhood, Josep shared his father's staunch republican and socialist views and was politically fluent enough at such a young age to discuss the character of the new Republic with his family. While appreciating its efforts, he recalled, it was clear even in 1931 that the Republican government was struggling to consolidate itself against the old elites. The threat of confrontation with Spain's economic, military and religious establishment would grow year upon year, with bitter workers' uprisings and far-right intrigues which created a general turbulence throughout Spain in the early Thirties.

But it was in July 1936 — half a year after the election of the Popular Front, a coalition consisting of liberal republicans, communists and social democrats — that General Francisco Franco attempted a military coup, and workers were compelled to finally rise up. As open, armed confrontation between the old and new Spain finally erupted, Josep and his brother Vicente volunteered for the workers' militias that had cobbled themselves together overnight to defend the Republic and destroy fascism. Initially seeking to join the armed forces of the Republican Left and then the Communist Party, the seventeen-year-old Josep was rejected on age grounds by the former, while the latter had no weapons for new militiamen. After falsifying his identification papers to add a few years to his age, Josep managed to join the Pablo Iglesias Column, which was organised by the Socialist Party. With his comrades, he left for the Teruel front on 13 September 1936, where they fought to aid the republican defence of Madrid. After several years of fighting across the country, Josep was badly wounded by shrapnel in 1938.

While in recovery, Josep presented himself to the 129th International Brigade as a French national. As one of the most geographically dispersed formations of those who had defied international law and risked losing their national citizenship to defend the Republic, the 129th was nicknamed the "forty nations brigade". While serving as a French translator as well as a regular soldier, Josep would later say that his comrades were so diverse that most knew each other by nationality before name, and he counted among his unit men from Canada, China, Cuba, France, Germany, the Netherlands and Switzerland, among others.

Yet despite the best efforts of these volunteers — and of the republican people themselves — democracy in Spain was in retreat. The collective refusal of Western democracies to aid their beleaguered neighbour saw the democratic forces deprived of desperately needed military hardware and medical supplies. Materiel from the Soviet Union and Mexico, a worldwide Aid for Spain movement and the collective mobilisation of the Spanish people and their international friends could not resist the military might of fascist armies from Germany, Italy and Portugal, who placed entire armies and air forces at Franco's disposal while Britain, France and America looked on.

In the misplaced hope that the Republic's international bargaining stance would be improved if they were perceived to be fighting a solely national war against non-domestic foes, it was decided that the International Brigades would be demobilised. After a tearful goodbye through Barcelona, thousands heard Dolores Ibárruri — the communist politician known for popularising the slogan *"no pasaran"* ("they shall not pass") during the defence of Madrid — tell them:

You can go proudly. You are history. You are legend. You are the heroic example of democracy's solidarity and universality in the face of the vile and accommodating spirit of those who interpret democratic principles with their eyes on hoards of wealth or corporate shares which they want to safeguard from all risk.

However, Josep did not leave with the International Brigades, nor with the 500,000 refugees who poured into France in early 1939. He returned to Alcàsser, where he was promptly arrested and sent to the Albatera concentration camp. Of the 200 concentration camps established by Franco, Albatera was the most important. At 700 metres long and 200 metres wide, Albatera had a population of around 15,000 socialists, trade unionists, writers and artists. Around 25,000 people died there, with many buried in anonymous mass graves on the site. Josep's captors forced him to witness mass executions of failed escapees, once telling *El País* that "I will never in my life forget the screams of the executed".

After being moved around other fascist jails, Josep was released in 1942. He showed no interest in accepting Franco's victory, however, throwing himself into building the illegal trade union movement and the armed struggle of the *maquis* in the mountains. In 1947, a tip-off was received that he was to be arrested and sentenced to death, and that a huge dossier had been compiled on him by the authorities. Crossing the Pyrenees on foot into France, Josep was eventually reunited with his brother, who had made the journey in 1939 with other republican soldiers, found himself inside the internment camp of Gurs with several *brigadistas* from Latin America, and ended up escaping to fight with the Resistance against Nazi occupation. When Franco's Spain received its admittance into the United Nations in 1955, Josep was given what he called a "sanctimonious" amnesty on his death sentence, pardoned on the condition that he would never return to Spain. His two *maquis* comrades were not so lucky: both had been caught and shot.

As several obituaries noted, Josep spent much of his later life passionately campaigning to uphold the memory of the Republic and those who fought to defend it. He would be present at every major event, draped in the red, yellow and purple *tricolor* more often than not, happy to speak to anyone and booming out republican songs like "Ay Carmela". He remained a committed communist and anti-fascist until his last breath: speaking to the *Guardian*, Almudena Cros, the president of the Association of the

Friends of the International Brigades, mentioned how joyfully he laughed when Franco was finally exhumed from the Valley of the Fallen, his tomb that had been built by republican slave labour.

With his passing, the memory of one of the most powerful demonstrations of universal brotherhood in history has slipped closer into oblivion. In a British context, this past year alone has seen newly published books about volunteers like Marguerite Addy, Howard "Andy" Andrews, Jimmy Higgins and James R. Jump. This renewal of interest should be encouraged, and not for the purposes of sentimentality or historic intrigue, but in the continuing struggle for a better future. The progressively minded may not show great concern for building on the long-term legacy of our cause, but our enemies certainly do — and all too keenly.

Indeed, when Walter Benjamin wrote that "even the dead will not be safe from the enemy if he is victorious", he easily could have been describing the efforts of the far-right — in and out of power — to silence the legacy of the anti-fascist struggle. When Polish *brigadistas* were commemorated in Warsaw in 2016, the event was attacked by fascists who hurled a smoke grenade at them — and on the grenade was inscribed "*ha pasado*" ("we have passed"). In Memento Park, Hungary's national park which claims to warn of the "dangers of authoritarianism", monuments stand to the International Brigades and Miklós Steinmetz, a Spanish volunteer who died liberating Budapest from Nazi occupation. And in July 2011, members of the Workers' Youth League — the Norwegian Labour Party's youth wing — gathered on the island of Utøya to unveil a plaque to four young comrades of theirs who had died in Spain. Four days later, sixty-nine of them were murdered, in what was the largest far-right atrocity in Europe since 1945.

These are ominous reminders that the legacy of the International Brigades must be reaffirmed. Not only their heroism and idealism, but their discipline, their sense of belonging to a cause so much greater than themselves as individuals, and their collective resolve to act coherently for the ultimate victory of that cause. As the human race edges towards oblivion, progressives are doing future generations a great disservice if they allow it to be forgotten that there once were mass movements that could produce people such as those who joined the International Brigades. Despite the best efforts of the far right, those who fought for the Spanish Republic were one of the few defeated peoples to have emerged as victors in the battle of historical memory. But now there no longer exists a single human who once swelled the ranks of the International Brigades, and so it is down to us to maintain that victory, and to rebuild the sort of movement that created people like Josep Almudéver Mateu.

TRINIDAD / PATRICK A. HOWELL & CHRISTIAN W. HOWELL

"There is a voice that doesn't use words. Listen."
— Rumi

Trinidad is a great spirit. Truly great. But for now, we lie on an emergency room hospital floor in the early hours. It's cold — so cold. And we are in pain, and in so many ways, lower than we have ever been. Might as well be ants. And the room partition, a towering skyscraper — this is an epic worldwide depression extinction scenario level event. *Trinidad is leaving us and will soon be gone.* Memories of his serendipitous spirit of love magic, sweet joy and big love swirl around us. We share photos and videos of our lives together — drop-offs and pick-ups at school, running wild in the park — lying and just chilling in bed, watching Netflix or lazy time in the family atrium-foyer. He groans, not so much in pain but resigned to a strange fate — he will no longer be with us, his family, by the time this morning has passed. He has been our best friend. A counsellor. A psychotherapist. A ridiculous adventurer. And in a home of sociopathic competitive spirits, he is the greatest athlete... by far. He is also the most spiritually fluent — speaking principles such as hope, faith and kindness effortlessly. Trinidad is a love-master. A super soul. *Our hero.*

It's sunny outside, birds are singing in full orchestral arrangement in our oceanside bedroom community; the sun is brighter than it has been in quite some time, heralding a season of uncommon brilliance and beauty; the Carlsbad wind is charged with a soft subtle blue reminding us of the COVID-19 season we have all come through.

It's all horribly ironic. I lost my father two years earlier, and my son Christian lost his grandfather. Matter of fact, after forty-eight years on the planet, it was the first time I had lost anyone in my life so close to me. Yes, in the midst of COVID-19 season, when millions of folks have had tribulation inflicted by the worst pandemic in a century, I seem to have found a way to honour my pain. And that is what makes Trinidad so great — never thinking about himself, engaging in the sickness of spirit life that is ego. His was a spirit that spoke without ever uttering a single syllable. And soon it will be his time to move on. And this life will go on.

Trinidad loves that — that basic "it is what it is" analysis. As D.H. Lawrence blacked in ink so eloquently, "*I never saw a wild thing sorry for itself.* A small bird will drop frozen dead from a bough without ever having felt sorry for itself." Trinidad's is the soul that expressed simply by being. Sure, Eckhart Tolle, Deepak Chopra, Mooji and Maharishi Mahesh Yogi are *the teachers.* Trinidad and his kind, however, are *the masters* — magical as all spirits from the realm of the mystical and enchanted. And now that he is leaving, we all realise a hole is opening up in us and feel the gaping wound that will be left in his absence. That hole is the size of loss and the dark pull of gravity where your soul takes on the dimensional weight of epic loss. Call it depression. He never takes anything to heart. Like D.H. said, I never saw him feel sorry for himself. Even as Chris and I had become master tormentors who would return his unbounded love with our unique brand of sly-smiled mischief. Chris would blow in his ears or I would pull his knuckles and he would bare teeth, his lip curling in contempt, revealing a jagged incisor — the equivalent of *Scarface*'s Tony Montana's heart-stopping loco stare — and we would laugh and call him Snaggletooth.

Trinidad, the splendid soul; a creative love whose thoughts are never far from the present moment and how to just *be*. He is our brother. A master of agape; unabashed in exemplifying the spirit of universal love. He has a profound understanding of our all too human existence as emotional beings. His EQ is radioactive and universal like Professor Charles Xavier's telepathy. When we are feeling down or lonely, he will always hug and console us. And in his characteristic slip-slap way, machine-spray-gun kisses, peppering one of us or whoever is there with an unbounded spirit expressing the inexpressible. Whenever we play ball, he will tackle us and run away with the ball and we all end up wrestling over it in a deadly epic battle. He gnashes his teeth and furrows his brow, hollering violently. We laugh, ever the tormentors and as great a psychological competitor — winning is everything to him. *But it is winning in life.* Despite a diminutive size, he is a champion. Pure champ with a fourteen-carat gold and blue-ribbon pedigree. After wrestling over the ball for a while, we make up and have dinner. How Trinidad loves his chicken and beef — like a real Caribbean man, he sinks his teeth into the bone, no matter how large, and sucks the marrow until all that is left are splinters. *Carpe diem!* After dinner, we watch a movie together, although he always seems more interested in his hygiene or birds that fly by the window.

We called him "Trinidad" because he is an erudite fellow. Also, a master of himself, his emotional IQ is cosmic... But I said that already, didn't I? The small boot-shaped Caribbean island called Trinidad is off the coast of Venezuela, an ancestral home with a tribe of people who are as distinct as they are brilliant. The people are spirit-rich bee-jeez-zillionaires. Just like our people, our Trinidad is a psychotic *loco* too. That's Spanglish for a hoop-and-a-hollering psycho maniac fun-loving freak. Skating down the stairway triple-time, that pompous butt-in-the-air walk, the huge mile-long-tongue smile — which is to say he knows no bounds — jumps in your arms, on your back, and peppers your face, neck, nose, eyes, ears with sweet kisses, each one of them filled with a liquid Hershey's kiss of freedom or unadulterated joy. But I already said that, didn't I? You would smile, against every inborn instinct of integrity or guarding the primacy of your person. You smile because he can transform his being into one of pure joy and delight. Trinidad is a *charismatic* — filled with the great spirit. And the molecules in his body affect your own. Trinidad is the spirit of love magic.

Three days ago, we were going for a walk in our neighbourhood, and as usual, he would explore the bush scents or admire birds in a daylight sky. While we were walking, a rottweiler beast bolted out of its garage, broke leash with its owner and savagely sunk its teeth into Trinidad's neck. Savage Mongoloid Villain picked him up and started flinging him around like he was a ragdoll. He didn't stop until I put him into a chokehold and squeezed his trachea. When Demented Rage Beast finally let go, there were bite wounds on both sides of Trinidad's neck and one on his chest. We rushed him to the emergency room where they gave him painkillers and told us that the bites on his neck were three centimetres away from a blood vessel and that he was lucky to be alive. *It wasn't luck —* Trinidad is a fighter from the spirit realm. We left him at the hospital for the night and would pick him up the next morning. The wounds were fatal, his skin deformed black and leathery, a patch of rotting blood everywhere he laid to rest from the pain. His face bloated with bruising and blood from the incident. He has to be put to sleep. The doctor has prepared long syringes — one that has stopped his heart and another that has ended his suffering.

See — *love magic* is he chose us. We first met at the Carlsbad rescue shelter, roaming isles of lost dogs looking to transition into a home. On our seven visits, he campaigned with his infectious enthusiasm and slowly enchanted us with his special spell of magic. When we walked past him, he would start jumping up and down and got on his hind legs and trotting like Rocket Raccoon, with whom he shares an uncanny resemblance. We asked if we could play with him and see if he was a good dog, and after that we knew he was the one. When he came home with us, he couldn't stop running in the backseat of our car like a maniac — after all, we had all won. *Trinidad is concentrated, unadulterated love magic.*

After Trinidad became a part of our family, everything changed. Less than two weeks after coming home, however, we took a hike on the Calavera Hills behind our house. We were at the mighty incline, surrounded by wildlife, bird compositions and the vastness of the world, almost at a ninety-degree angle toiling up a hell hill. Calavera is a dormant 5000-year-old volcano with lake caves, labyrinths and a plug that contains a fine-basalt that clogged the volcano's throat millions of years ago. The devil himself — Mephistopheles — came down that hill from the hell unbounded, barrelling at over twenty-five miles per hour. And Trinidad, a pup, bolted, leaving us alone to face the mountain biker. Trinidad, gone! Christian was brokenhearted. He had lost his best friend before the friending began. We called and searched everywhere for Trinidad over two hours as we walked the three miles home and it became dark. When we got home, Trinidad was in the front yard burrowing a hole, and looked at us as if to say, "What took you so long my Gs? I almost made it to China. When you see the devil, right? Run for home!" That's *love magic*.

Trinidad always knew when something was wrong, like a beacon from the universe. And he could take the low negative frequencies and convert them into his special love magic. He knew when something was off. He sensed when you were having a bad day. He was the only one attuned to everyone at any given time. He would just come and check in on you. *From nowhere.* Rub his wet nose under your hand. Squeeze his body under the circumference of your belly. Lay a paw on your thigh and look at you lovingly, standing erect on his hinds. Tap your soul. Fix the pain. Spark you new. Love dripping in. Trinidad — that's our love magic.

We lost one of our good friends today, perhaps a bestie (def. not a beastie) — Trinidad, a Jack Russell Fox Terrier who is a good soul, a bright light, a brilliant spirit; a master empath and better than most. He never faltered in loving completely and truly. He was so good at it. Oftentimes, he was the one who could get along with everyone, which on its face seems like such a simple quality but is truly the mark of an evolved humanity and being. We learned from him how to be free, free to love, forgiving, let go, go with the flow, to just be, take pleasure in all that life is (not just lofty ambitions) and how to always give love. *How to be love.*

Who is going to do those things now? Who's going to do the love magic? It became a part of our blessing. It became a part of our lifestyle. Our fortune. He really tended to our emotional needs daily. When we felt uneasy. When we felt ill. "I'm here," he would say, without uttering so much as a word. Just his presence was enough. *Amor magia.*

He left the world — our world — better. Trinidad was our family's love magic. Three cheers to the Jack Russell Fox Terrier that was our pet. But really, he was so much more than that. I think you get that though. *He is our hero. Our love magic.*

ERIC CANTONA / JOE KENNEDY

For the whole of the first decade of the twenty-first century, I played in a band. After a few years, I became the singer, but at first, I just stood at the front of the stage and made my guitar rattle and squeal. A couple of hours before our first show, so before I was the official frontman, some of us were sitting in our bassist's kitchen drinking Pimm's from greasy pint glasses. I must have said something about feeling nervous because the bassist, still a good friend, told me that I had "a lot of presence", something our Bavarian vocalist-at-the-time, who could be very blunt, immediately shook her head at and said, "no you don't".

Since then — and if I ever did have it, I've surely much less of it now — I have been quite interested in this concept of presence, by what people mean when they use it. Sometimes it is used as a slack synonym for a sort of wrong comeliness, sometimes, with a higher level of abstraction, to denote an anchor-point for something which is not quite, but also not not, desire.

Yet I think really there's another evaluation posited by the word which, one might add, is contextually noun-locked, something one *has* but cannot adjectivally *be*: saying something is "present" is not the same as saying it "has presence". If someone "has presence" in our judgement, what we are doing is speculating as to how they feel about, in, and most importantly *as* themselves; they, we fancy, experience themselves as located exactly *where we see them* and *when we see them*, as geotemporally tethered, as in their place — which is wherever they happen to be at the time. It's exactly what I don't have when I'm standing just to one side of the barber's plate window or over the road from a shop I've never been in before, Prufrocking.

And nobody could ever speak of *themselves* as being the possessor of presence. Given its connotations of self-reliance, of being sustained by the internal forces of its own style, the irony of "presence" is that it is only ever attributed and suppositioned. In my lifetime, and certainly in that period in this country, few have been more frequently assumed to have it than Eric Cantona, the Frenchman who played as a centre-forward in England's top division for Leeds and Manchester United for a mere five years before retiring young to become an actor, beach footballer and emblem of a certain kind of caprine good living.

I grew up supporting Darlington, my birth-town team, but I've long been a Manchester United sympathiser as well. Even before Cantona signed and the club began to overpower English football, there was something about the type of volcanically aggressive players Alex Ferguson signed, the sweeping violence of his side's counterattack, the blood-redness of the shirts, that engaged the fantasy life of a shy, nervous kid. In autumn 1992, when Ferguson made a black op over the Pennines to steal Leeds' figurehead in circumstances whose official secrets have never fully been disclosed, I had just started secondary school. I had developed a lisp. I chewed through fountain pen cartridges in class and came home with ink running down my chin, onto my collar and tie. I'd retrieved the old Transformers toys out of the box they'd gone into when I was seven. I was entirely inside myself, and yet entirely without presence.

The first thing that made Cantona *mine* was in fact the nature of his arrival at Old Trafford itself. I come from County Durham, but my family had moved to North Yorkshire, only eight territorial miles away but much more than that attitudinally. The town we moved to was beautiful geographically, spilling down a hillside on the very edge of the eastern Pennines, and architecturally, with Georgian public buildings and alleyways of little cottages winding beneath a Norman castle. The Prince of Wales claimed it was the "Siena of the North". But I remember the fog in the playground on my first day of school and the different, flintier accents, and even the children had their backs up, knowing what they liked and liking what they knew, full of the superiority bred of the certainty that one's suspicions are healthy. A few years later, by the time I started secondary, Leeds United were the champions of England and half the school, and definitely more than half of the teachers, supported them with smarmy chauvinism. The club's brittle, cornered mentality and tight-fisted playing style were representative of all the things that made the north-easterner in me uneasy in Yorkshire: Cantona's mode of departure — not, sadly, across the River Tees to Darlington — felt like a calculated, hilarious prod in the eye for the county.

Even after that, his ascendancy in my approval was for a long time not really to do with how he played as such. He seemed to improve United just by being around the place, and his poster (from which I learned his middle names and his date of birth but was misled by an unfact-checked claim that he was born in Paris rather than Marseille) brought my otherwise messy room together. My mum started to call him "Eric". The summer after United won the first of their doubles under Ferguson, we travelled to Auxerre, where he'd begun his career, and went unexpectantly upstairs in a small backstreet pizzeria only to discover from the thickets of memorabilia that it was one he'd frequented in the mid-Eighties. A couple of nights later, in a humid motel, we watched United play Rangers in a pre-season friendly on French TV, switching on late in the game in time to see Cantona sent off for his usual crime of belligerent, inaccurate tackling. It was the first time I'd really felt personally affronted by one of his dismissals, but, and we all know what comes next, of course, it wasn't to be the last.

There isn't a great deal left to say about what happened between Cantona and Crystal Palace fan Matthew Simmons at Selhurst Park in the late winter of 1995. I mean, there is something *I would like to say* about it, but it would be a lie: that I learned from it that you should never allow yourself to be bullied, that you should never tolerate an imposition, that justice must always be delivered and so on. I've derived pleasure from imagining what it felt like to be Simmons at the exact moment Cantona came for him, of picturing how time must have slowed to the extent that he'd be coping simultaneously not only with his sudden realisation that the guy he'd just called a motherfucker was not about to let the insult go, but also with the pricking awareness that he was going to become negatively famous, forever. Retrospectively, it feels like a good fable about people getting what they deserve, but, if truth be told, the thing I should have taken from it straight away was not what I actually did take from it.

Yet there's that presence again. On the Simmons-cam, what is seen is someone who is completely there in what they're doing, who is outside any logic of consequence and therefore the worst person to have recently called a motherfucker. This relates to how Cantona actually played football. Go back and watch the videos and, in a way, there is something inelegant and angularly gross about Cantona's physical movement: his turns had too many points, the way he brought a high ball down was exaggerated and contorted. Every unique poise within an instance of technique seemed to be legible, as though you were observing a zoetrope as it slowed. Watching a vaguely comparable creative player, Dennis Bergkamp, say, or Zinedine Zidane, one struggles to parse the technique, to map its constitutive dispositions. Cantona's corporeal workflow, on the other hand, could be quite simply reproduced as a flowchart, as a list of things which just were going to occur, regardless of how they appeared externally.

His style might have been seen as clunky, but it could also be regarded as modernist, a making-the-stone-stony, Shklovskian football. The key dialectic of modernist art, from the Symbolists — like Rimbaud, who Cantona apparently loved — onwards was between transcoded meaning and absolute presence, between Freud's proliferating phalluses-in-disguise and Freud's cigar-which-was-just-a-cigar. The latter, the just-cigar, tends to be underprivileged in Anglophone discussions about modernism, which is why everyone spends so much time fretting about what Kafka's castle is supposed to be a metaphor for, or Dali's clocks, or the lighthouse nobody can go to until the weather is just-so. Likewise, Cantona became the first Nineties footballer (but not the last, bearing in mind what happened to his sometime protégé David Beckham) to become a source of angst about what he *meant* or what he could tell us about masculinity, while everyone overlooked his unusual level of there-ness.

Unable to reproduce this presence on my own behalf, my Cantona preoccupation could only be played out imitatively in the realm of things he meant or was supposed to mean. I turned my collar up while playing football. I acquired an underexamined belief in the aesthetic and intellectual superiority of France, the short-term effect of which was a quite surprising A in my French GCSE, but which in the long-term mutated into an academic interest in structuralism, post-structuralism and the *nouveau roman*. I wrote my Master's thesis on Julia Kristeva and Alain Robbe-Grillet, ridiculously. In other words, I went to university and became fascinated by the undoing of the whole idea of presence and intrinsic meaning, but when I started to teach this stuff, or give presentations — *present*-ations, as a less self-conscious deconstructionist would perhaps pun — on it, I had to Canton-ise myself; to, honestly, go through "what would Eric do?" processes to put myself in front of people in the first place. Clearly, I have never quite lost my faith in presence through any number of attempts to dissemble it.

From time to time, I tell myself that it's probably time to grow out of this infantile idolisation: I am very nearly forty, and I can stand in front of a lecture theatre or address a conference with little to no anxiety now. It isn't as though I track Cantona's post-football career, particularly, although from afar much of it looks quite cynically advertorial. Honestly, though, I'm highly unlikely to: it seems necessary, even if I don't really believe in the concept most of the time, to attribute presence somewhere, to allow myself this lapse.

DEVILS / MATTEO MANDARINI

I want to draw a distinction between the *hērōs* and the modern hero. The former were demi-gods, super-human, which, while they cannot be divorced from a purported (though mythical) historical existence, cannot be reduced to that "historicity" without — as the great mythologist and philologist Carl (Károly) Kerényi writes — "forfeit[ing] thereby their mythological aspect, which connects them with the gods and by virtue of which they, like the gods, act as Prototypes". But we can say that, in many ways, it is their hyper-humanity that makes of such figures *demi-*gods, without their ever ceasing to be recognisably human — even once they join the gods.

In contrast, the modern hero I want to recall here is the one who is always already *in-*human. That is to say, heroes are those that somehow fail to become human or, because of their depravity, cannot but be outside all human norms. The term "anti-hero" falls short, in that it fails to remark what is truly novel in this figure, as I hope to explain. The reason why Churchill cannot be a hero in this modern sense, is because he "succeeded" — in his military victories (as in his racial violence) — and so finds himself utterly within the common run of things, someone to whom others might aspire because of "achievements", recognised, affirmed, even comforting.

Few have been able, like Dostoyevsky, to see the modern hero for what he is, for what she is: someone who escapes all possible praise, who defiantly refuses all acknowledgment.

Nietzsche approaches this same insight — but falls short. He fails, because he *celebrates* the hero, the "blonde beast". While he glimpses the hero's excessiveness, he domesticates it again by calling for him (it was always "he" for Nietzsche) to invent and establish a new scale or table of values. In contrast, Dostoyevsky accepts the scale; he places the hero outside it, in the same way as he accepted and affirmed the God in which he could not believe. God is value. Outside of God, where the hero dwells, "everything is permitted". Thus, Dostoyevsky, unable to believe in Value, despite all his efforts, stands outside the scale to which he submits. Unlike his "heroes", he submits. But he does not believe. The hero then stands outside Value, to which she does not submit, and is monstrous, a monstrousness to which the hero belongs, beyond censure, beyond compare, outside valuation. Value is the enemy of modern heroism, contrasting with the ancient hero who is such because of a particular kingly *krátos* (power) bestowed by the gods.

The modern hero is heroic in divestment. Divestment of all human qualities. In the "failure" of humanity, either of exemplifying humanity or persisting in it. There must be something despicable about the hero. By way of counterpoint, consider Prince Myshkin, the Christ-like protagonist of *The Idiot*. Here we have a demi-god of the Christian era, where the human is in its — near — perfect form. But Myshkin is not a hero, in the sense I am discussing here, any more than Christ is. It is precisely the extreme humanity of Christ, as of Myshkin — their being human-all-too-human — that makes of them gods. The events surrounding the Passion culminating in the Resurrection may seal Christ's divinity, but it is his exemplary humanity that led him there. Dostoyevsky's heroes are exemplary of nothing, if not inhumanity. It is only those able to submit finally to Christ that (re-)gain their humanity by submitting to the scale of values that, finally confirming it, share in the divine (I am thinking, of course, of the disappointing and yet necessary conclusion of Raskolnikov's story). The human, then, ceases to be a hero in becoming a demi-god, in submitting to Value.

There are, of course, many different depictions of such heroes in the modern novel. Not all contain *alkē* (valour). Neither do they exemplify, as the great structural linguist Émile Benveniste has it in his rendering of the term in the *Dictionary of Indo-European Concepts and Society*, the *kraterós*, the hardness, brutality or violence of a Nikolai Stavrogin — "Dostoyevsky's greatest artistic creation", in Konstantin Mochulskii's words. In Josef K., we have a figure always outside the Law, standing in a place *before* access to Law, to Value. This is not a temporal, chronological "before", but a logical one that precludes its comprehension, for K. stands outside the sense-giving division of "lawful" and "unlawful" that only becomes valid once *under* the Law. It thus marks an inability, unfittingness, incapacity to submit to Law, however much, in contrast to Stavrogin, K. may long to submit. Perhaps K. finds himself closer to Dostoyevsky himself, who stands before a God in whom he cannot believe. Submitting himself to an absence that forever precludes him from gaining access to the divine. But whereas Dostoyevsky recognises the Godly, that is, he recognises Law (and so the unlawful), for K. there is nothing to be recognised, for the Law confronts him always as mysterious, enigmatic, alien. The brutality is reversed;

the Value from which he is excluded is experienced as always-already unattainable but instantiated and active in the world. It thus presents itself as a brutal, unintelligible violence. K. will forever stand outside a Law that threatens him. This is his heroic standpoint. Equally, Stavrogin stands outside, although unlike K. he senses the Law through the equivalence of pleasure he derives from virtue as from vice; but while, again unlike K., he has an experience of the Law, it is one marked by a fundamental indiscernibility, taking pleasure in both vice and virtue. Law is thus as enigmatic for him as it is for Josef K.

I do not wish to suggest that psychoanalytic readings (or theological ones, for that matter) of figures such as Stavrogin or Josef K. are invalid. It is perfectly possible to go some way to explaining Stavrogin's character through an account of Varvara Petrovna's narcissistic mothering. A full analysis of the motives — conscious or otherwise — of such figures is, of course, entirely legitimate. But Stavrogin and K. exceed such psychoanalytic reductions; they cannot be captured by such "reaction formations". They are necessarily greater than the sum of their explanatory reductions, for what such figures exemplify is a quality that in somehow marking them out as *in*-human — where the prefix marks a negation, a not, placing them outside the human understood as a set of values, of exclusion-inclusions (e.g. Law/Lawless) — situates them as unique points prior to decision (here Beckett's "heroes" mimic Kafka's), rather than following upon a decision that consigns them to the ready-made trajectory of the Law, Virtue, Meaning.

None of these "heroes" can be eulogised, but for different reasons. The in-humanity of Kafka's heroes sees them dying like dogs (as in the end of *The Trial*), or as an insect, an *ungeheures Ungeziefer*, or monstrous unclean insect (*Metamorphosis*). Stavrogin's inhuman brutality approaches the bloodlust of Ares, the god of war, hated by his own parents, Zeus and Hera (what human child could be so hated by their parents?). Whereas Benveniste writes, the term *krátos* (the power of a king) is used solely for gods and humans, the adjective *kratéros* can have two meanings: on the one hand, as the magnificence of being "provided with *krátos*" and, on the other, as the "far from complimentary" (Benveniste) sense of hard, cruel, violent, applied as much to people as to animals and things. It is the term used by Hecuba, for instance, when she turns on Achilles, who has just killed her favourite son Hector and dragged his body around the walls of Troy. It is fitting too for Stavrogin, endowed with a boundless cruelty — inhuman in its coldness. We might think of one last modern heroic monster, this time a collective one that was identified by another thinker whose lifespan coincided almost exactly with that of Dostoyevsky (1821-1881): Karl Marx (1818-1883). The proletariat are the product of the expansion of capitalist industry, produced as the lowest of the low, their families torn asunder, without nation, divorced from their very activity by their total alienation, without a culture of their own and without all elements that make a society human, and so, without the common condition of humanity — *in*-human, we might say — they have nothing to lose but the ties to their conditions of existence. They do not possess the elements of a new society, just the brutal need, the *kratéros* perhaps, to destroy the present one.

I am aware that there is a perhaps certain coldness (not

to say cruelty) to this apparently impersonal (not to say perverse) idea of "heroism", where the "hero" stands back and observes as if from afar their own failed humanity. It is as if Stavorgin stands aloof and observes his own actions with a detachment that makes the cruelty all the more dreadful. K. too, though desperate to have access to the Law, is caught in a no man's land of inaction, where he can but wait and wonder, compelled to meditate on his own failure. Even Dostoyevsky himself, though aching for the God in which he cannot believe, can only linger unhappily, and observe the world in which people of unfailing goodness act at a distance from their God that all too often seems to forsake them, or where others act with the brutality of a world where "everything is permitted". In all cases the actor is divorced from her actions in a world in which she is not at home (*heimlich*), a world that is uncanny (*unheimlich*) into which she is thrown (Freud famously plays on the dichotomy between the homely and uncanny). If I ask myself the reason for my fascination with these figures, I might intellectualise and accuse the inevitable (and inescapable) alienation of capitalist society that installs a gap between action and realization, where desires never quite seem to be one's own, and beliefs are chosen from an ever-expanding set of disposable "offerings". But there is surely more to it than that. Why would a rabid Marxist atheist be attracted to a figure who longs for God and whose politics are a reactionary blend of anti-socialism and belief in the Russian Orthodox Church to realise the Kingdom of God on Earth? Perhaps it is precisely the wilfulness of his belief, held in the face of the absence of the ultimate ground that might found it, i.e., God, that attracts me. A decision to believe without ground, without home, with the consequent failed sense of self where one can never quite believe one's own actions, words, beliefs, for they lack ground. Reclaiming such a figure is perhaps a way to try to assert a certain heroism inhering in the mere fact of existing upon such an absent ground.

The Waldsiedlung or Forest Estate, Berlin. Photograph by the author.

BRUNO TAUT / OWEN HATHERLEY

There were all kinds of ways to be a "heroic architect" in the twentieth century. The most famous comes from a sort of amalgam of Le Corbusier, Frank Lloyd Wright and Ayn Rand's fictional Howard Roark in *The Fountainhead* — a driven, maniacal genius who will achieve the form in his head in gigantic three dimensions and do so Whatever! The! Cost! This is clearly pernicious and endures today in the form of the cults around people like Frank Gehry, Peter Zumthor or the late Zaha Hadid: the great form-givers, artists in steel and concrete, for whom the end user and, even more so, the worker, is the greatest irrelevance. Another is the architect as mere instrument of the Zeitgeist, a vessel or a medium through which technology speaks, a model that links Walter Gropius, Buckminster Fuller and Norman Foster; whether you find this attractive perhaps depends on how much you find the spirit of the time particularly admirable.

While these are easy models of heroism to criticise, and have been, repeatedly, the most fashionable model today is irritating in its own way. That is, the architect as self-abnegator — from Walter Segal to Alejandro Aravena, the engaged expert who merely gives "tools" to allegedly spontaneously forming communities who then do the actual construction and much of the design themselves, as if the most important thing the architect can do is avoid making buildings, instead acting as a mere facilitator for the creation of usually very conventional spaces. Like

Jacques Rancière's "Ignorant Schoolmaster", the teacher who knows that to teach is oppressive, this is the architect who sees architecture itself as a system of domination. These ideas can achieve some good results — Segal's self-build houses are clearly lovely to live in — but it is too often an ideology of middle-class guilt, and one which denies "ordinary people" the possibility of understanding or enjoying the spaces and textures of a real, fully realised work of architecture.

In between, there's a whole set of strategies, many of them based on the deep interlinking of architecture and politics that happened between the late nineteenth century and the 1970s. This always rested on the question of how the designer preserved their ideals in the face of the major political movements of the time, and it could take all sorts of forms. Moisei Ginzburg was committed to a modern architecture for Soviet communism and was heartbroken when the Soviets rejected it; Giuseppe Terragni believed fiercely in modernism as the appropriate style for Italian fascism; Le Corbusier or Mies van der Rohe preserved their integrity as fiercely original designers while pimping their designs out to anyone from socialists to fascists to industrialists; while someone like Alexey Shchusev would cheerfully design in any style for any client, whether it was a Byzantine monastery for the Orthodox Church, a constructivist office block for the Bolsheviks, or a classical palace for the KGB. None of these seem to me entirely "heroic", but if there is one of the great modern architects whose example I think is genuinely impeccable, a genuine model of how to work, how to design, and how to build in the world that exists, it is Bruno Taut, who worked in

Germany, the USSR, Japan and finally Turkey between the 1910s and 1930s.

Taut is in a strange position in the history of modern architecture. A major figure in the 1920s and early 1930s, his work was gradually written out of the story after 1933 (Mies and Le Corbusier disliked his use of bright colours), and only reclaimed from the 1970s onwards. For an English reader, much of his voluminous writing has been translated, mainly in the 1970s and 1980s, but none of it is in print, unlike that of his contemporaries such as Loos, Mies, Corbusier and Gropius. His major works, a series of social housing estates in the outlying districts of Berlin, are so well respected that they form part of a UNESCO World Heritage listing, but they have never become part of the Berlin hipster itinerary, remaining quiet, suburban and rather "normie". You have to piece the story together in the library, both from his translated texts and from the scattered writings on the man, some of which, like those by Iain Boyd-White and Esra Akcan, reveal a way of doing modern architecture that is very different to the respective ideals of the Howard Roark testosterone-driven genius, the cool Zeitgeist technician or the libertarian Ignorant School-architect. He had no allegiance to anything so silly as a single style or approach for every possible site — his principles were of a different order.

Taut was born in 1918 into a middle-class Jewish family in Königsberg, a peripheral East Prussian city which was absorbed into the Soviet Union after 1945, and now forms the main part of the Russian exclave of Kaliningrad. On becoming an architect, he entered a German architectural culture that had developed, via the British Arts and Crafts movement, a fixation on garden cities, but also its own more technocratic closeness to industry, technology and planning. His earliest works would follow these fixations but take them in increasingly weird directions. So, for instance, his first major garden suburb project, the Falkenberg estate on the outskirts of eastern Berlin, is planned like a Letchworth or a New Earswick, but abandoned completely the idea that these buildings should have a rough, tweedy integrity — instead, Taut planned a colour scheme inspired by Fauvist and Expressionist painting, introducing an artificiality and uncomplicated joy into what could otherwise look rather conservative. In 1914, meanwhile, he designed the famous Glass Pavilion at a trade fair in Cologne, in collaboration with the science-fiction writer Paul Scheerbart, who added some verses for the project. Although this is often described as a precursor of the glass and steel architecture of the post-war office city, glass for Taut and Scheerbart was not meant to be merely sleek or transparent — it was treated like glass in medieval cathedrals, illuminated and stained in multiple colours ("coloured glass destroys hatred", claimed Scheerbart's slogans on the walls). These already show someone pushing at the limits of what was possible at the time, from reformism and technocracy into increasingly utopian visions.

As the First World War dragged on, ending with the German Revolution of November 1918, these visions took over Taut's work. He opposed the war early on, welcomed the Russian Revolution and supported the Independent Social Democratic Party (USPD), which split from the official majority in opposition to the war, and would in 1920 merge with the Communist Party. But his response to the carnage was, apparently strangely, to dream of an alternative architecture of international community and communality. Between 1917 and 1919 he published *The City Crown*, *The Dissolution of Cities* and *Alpine Architecture*, all of which imagined a total, revolutionary reconstruction of the built environment around crystalline, almost Gothic steel and glass communal buildings, like his Glass Pavilion massively expanded; buildings which, while using the most modern technologies, were intended to be magical and fantastical. These came directly out of Taut's enthusiasm for the revolutions in Petrograd and Berlin, and were, as he saw them, a means of realising the *Communist Manifesto*'s demand for a dissolving of the divide between city and country. He also avidly set up various associations and collectives to propagate these ideas and new forms, whether through politicised artists' groups like the November Group and the Workers' Council for Art, and through a sort of secret society of utopian architects, the "Glass Chain".

When it became obvious that none of this was actually going to happen, and the revolutionary energy dissipated, Taut didn't opt, as so many did, for going apolitical or chasing commissions for business clients and private houses. Instead, as the German left settled for trying to gradually legislate socialism into existence, mainly through the work of urban local authorities, Taut put himself in their service. First in Magdeburg, he was appointed as city architect by the socialist mayor; most of what he achieved was a matter of working with what already existed, replicating his approach in the Falkenberg estate by painting nineteenth-century tenements in pulsating colours. Better remembered is what he then went on to do in Berlin, where he became the main architect of GEHAG, a trade union building society. GEHAG were offered by Berlin's socialist planner

Martin Wagner large swathes of the suburbs upon which to build new estates. Working with Wagner and the landscape architect Leberecht Migge, Taut designed four housing estates that mark an early peak in modernist housing — around three decades before large-scale modernist mass housing for a working class, politically engaged client rather than the *cognoscenti*, would reach the UK.

These Berlin estates, all of which are in very good condition and can easily be visited today, were built incrementally between 1924 and 1930 — Schillerpark, in the city's north; the Horseshoe Estate in Neukölln; the Forest estate (also rather unfortunately known by the name of a local pub, Uncle Tom's Cabin) in Zehlendorf; and the Carl Legien Estate, named after a trade union leader and the only one in the inner-city, in Prenzlauer Berg. They were built straightforwardly, usually of brick and only occasionally using concrete, which was then rendered in Taut's distinctive colours, which by now were influenced by the geometric emphases of modernist art movements like De Stijl or constructivism, though rejecting their puritan insistence on primary colours in favour of still lurid purples, greens, and in the famous "Red Front" of the Horseshoe Estate, an ostentatious use of the deep red of the people's flag. These terraced houses and tenement flats have none of Le Corbusier's "five points", and none of the structural display of Mies van der Rohe's work at the time in Barcelona and Brno, but it is difficult to imagine a more complete vision of what a socialist modern city could look like than the Forest estate in Zehlendorf, with its houses like three-dimensional El Lissitzky paintings, set in high pine trees — nature and technology in an extraordinary new unity that emphasises the strangeness of both. And while these houses were given clear "façades", in that their aesthetic comes from the paint as much as the materials, they followed the modernist demand that there be no back ends, no dark alleyways, no moment where cheapness and darkness can be found where you're not meant to be looking — every side of the house, Taut stressed, is the front of the house, and all of the houses were equal — no slum housing, no luxury housing.

Obviously, the rise of German fascism threatened an architect engaged in work like this; even irrespective of Taut's Jewish heritage, his houses were already considered "Un-German" in the 1920s, showing no interest whatsoever in the folkish qualities of German traditions — though the observant can easily see the influence of *Biedermeier* classical traditions in the proportions of these houses, they were deliberately anti-traditional in their aesthetic. Although he would not settle there, one of the first places where Taut tested the waters outside Germany was Britain. In a series of 1929 articles for the magazine *The Studio*, which were then collected as *Modern Architecture*, he explained to the English for the first time what Germans called "the New Building". Much like the Surrealists pointing out that the country of Lewis Carroll didn't need Parisians to bring them the surreal, Taut's approach was often to point out the way in which British life was already modernist, and gently push them away from the silliness and conservatism of the then-dominant Neo-Georgian. Perhaps part of my love for Taut comes from the fact that he did this by photographing Regency houses with grand, glassy circular bow windows in Southampton, my hometown, presumably the first place he stopped on the boat from Hamburg.

On the eve of the Nazi seizure of power, Taut escaped

to the Soviet Union, which had been, since the revolution, one of the major centres of the new architecture; he had been one of the first to showcase this at the turn of the 1920s in the magazine he edited, *Frühlicht*. Yet almost as soon as he moved to Moscow, the USSR shifted suddenly to neoclassical design, and Taut was unwilling to bend accordingly. Although he worked on town plans for some of the new industrial suburbs and cities for the Five-Year Plan, it may have been the only country where Taut worked that has no surviving buildings by him. Incredibly, he worked on an early version of the wedding cake Hotel Moskva by the Kremlin, which would be completed by his principle-free nemesis Alexey Shchusev. Like André Gide in his *Return from the USSR*, Taut said what he saw, and was very critical of the chaotic, corrupt and violent society he found in his time working in the country, but without veering into conventional anti-communism. What is probably more interesting is what happened to him next. Invited for a month's tour and lectures by a group of modernist architects in Tokyo, he ended up staying in Japan for three years; from there he would move to Turkey, where he died in 1938.

Taut's works in Berlin had veered suddenly from a utopian socialist dreamworld on paper, of giant collective glass houses on mountains, into a pragmatic but in many ways equally utopian series of workers' housing estates — linked by a continued commitment to equality, collectivity and some form of socialism, whether revolutionary or reformist. His work in Japan and Turkey shows how, unlike some socialists, he took his internationalism extremely seriously. Rather than doing a version of what he had designed in Berlin or Magdeburg, when he came to build in Atami, Ankara and Istanbul, he became obsessed with what Esra Akcan calls the "translation" of modernism into a new context. It couldn't and shouldn't be exactly the same in somewhere with different architectural traditions, different building materials, different nature and a different climate. He dedicated himself to a dual project of trying to propagandise for the "new building" and its social projects — collective housing estates in particular — and trying to learn about how architecture was produced in these countries, and what he could learn from it — a commitment to the cosmopolitan based on the idea that, as he put it, "human beings all over the world are endowed with an equal amount of reason".

Though the itinerary Berlin-Moscow-Tokyo-Istanbul seems more interesting today than the conventional route of Berlin-London-New York, the zealous could have criticised Taut in the 1930s for working enthusiastically for three authoritarian regimes — Stalinism, then a Japan committed to brutal imperial expansion and rapidly veering towards fascism, and ending with Ataturk's dictatorial secular modernising project (he would actually design the Turkish leader's *catafalque*). But with the possible exception of a stodgy university building in Ankara, none of this seems to have much affected his designs, which remained open and cosmopolitan, and explicitly opposed to any kind of nationalism. In Japan, Taut wrote a famous appreciation of the Katsura imperial villa in Kyoto in which he outlined how the values of 1920s modern architecture — lightweight construction, reproducibility, regularity, a flowing space where rooms melted into each other — could all be found in seventeenth-century Japan, centuries before "modernisation". His only surviving building in Japan, a villa in Atami, Shizuoka Province, is hard to categorise either as a modern building inspired by abstract painting or a traditional Japanese house, so much have the two been integrated.

Taut brought these all together in his last major work, his own house on the Bosphorus in the suburbs of Istanbul — a pagoda-like house raised on stilts above the trees, with a view of the exact point where Europe and Asia connect; it has a Turkish tiled roof, a 1920s Berlin modernist plate-glass window, and a logical wooden grid construction that is visibly Japanese but supported on giant concrete pillars. None of this is mere exotica, but rather an honest attempt, full of curiosity and invention, to meet a non-Western architecture on its own terms, in turn bringing to it what he has without being overbearing or patronising. In accordance with his will, when he died in 1938 at the age of fifty-eight from an asthma attack, this German Jewish socialist was buried in a Muslim cemetery. Unlike his peers, he never got round to glass office blocks in Manhattan or Park Lane offices for the Playboy Club. He lies elsewhere, representative of a socialist and internationalist modernism which retains all its power.

GILLIAN GODDARD / LESLEY-ANN BROWN

Gillian Goddard is a woman who, in her own words, wears many hats. She knows a lot about subjects I have only been contemplating — land, plants, history, oppression and so much more. During my stay in Trinidad, I would come to have many conversations with Goddard. I find her approach to life refreshing. She is not caught up in all of the middle-class trappings that seem to be all around me. She seems deeply committed to social change, and by the fruits of her labour, it's not all talk. Gillian Goddard is a brave activist who works in her community, a daring mother who refused to send her children to be institutionalised in a white supremacist school system, a woman who is applying solutions to local challenges, but most of all, she is a woman dedicated to her own growth and that of the community to which she belongs. For me, Gillian Goddard is more than a hero, she is a friend.

"Land is power, land is wealth, and, more importantly, land is about race and class. The relationship to land — who owns it, who works it and who cares for it — reflects obscene levels of inequality and legacies of colonialism and white supremacy in the United States, and also the world. Wealth accumulation always goes hand-in-hand with exploitation and dispossession."[1]

I've often wondered what my life would have looked like if my parents had not left the country of their birth, the

---

1 Nick Estes, "Bill Gates is the Biggest Private Owner of Farmland in the United States. Why?", *The Guardian*, 5 April 2021: https://www.theguardian.com/commentisfree/2021/apr/05/bill-gates-climate-crisis-farmland

twin-island nation of Trinidad and Tobago. If, rather than becoming immigrants in Brooklyn, New York, they had insisted on staying natives. But even that is a tenuous situation, as the descendants of enslaved Africans, indentured servants and subdued Caribs. What really is our land, our country, our nation, anyway? Nevertheless, it is the closest thing to home many of us have ever known.

What would my life have been like if they had passed down to me this citizenship, this right to claim nationhood of this former British colony (which was so much more even before that!), rather than give birth to me in a country foreign to them both and a new kind of empire? What if they had resisted the pull of modernity, first from rural to urban, then from motherland to imperial power; the draw from poverty to the (semi-)promise of becoming middle class (or appearing to be)? I am often left to lament the landlessness that further renders me, in my Black womanhood, so vulnerable.

An urbanite, born in Brooklyn, far from the country of my ancestors, I've often wondered what *the land* was like, the land that my ancestors once knew intimately and treated with a respect that is not allowed in our corporatized capitalist world. The land that some of them were forced to toil. But also, I know it wasn't all like that. I have some faint recollection of the loving alliance that was definitely once forged between them and the earth. No one on this planet would still be here if any of our ancestors were as thoughtless as our culture now seems to be, inherited from Europe, no less.

I often try to re-imagine what the landscape was like before colonisation. I think of the damming of the rivers as a metaphor for the damming of our memories. My great-grandmother was Carib, and although I do not remember her name, I know she is from the village of Sangre Grande, which I will soon learn from Gillian Goddard, the person I'm about to meet, means "Big Blood" — it was the scene of the largest war between the Caribs and the Spanish.

What were the plants used for medicine, like the bush tea my grandmother praised, the fruits and vegetables I grew up with like dasheen, bodi, guava...? It seems as if I know nothing about what is indigenous to this land and what was brought from far away.

It didn't seem that anyone I knew in Trinidad had access to land either, and even those that appeared to farmed industrially, not organically and in a rehabilitory fashion that I intuited was necessary given the extent agriculture had been implemented, from cocoa plantations to the growing of sugarcane. From former classmates to family, all seemed to live in suburbs, many of them gated, and locked their car doors as they spoke about "crime in Trinidad bad!" So, it was with a heavy heart that I sat at the side of my grandparents' home in Diamond Vale (that social experiment of concrete that seemed to harden our hearts towards our neighbours, eroding the spirit of communality and reciprocity that ensured our ancestors' survival), watching the pandemonium of parrots fly towards the sun that descended behind the hills that hugged the valley in which I found myself. I had been there to bury my grandmother, whom I would never see again, and was in a country that I had inherited from her but that seemed so far outside my reach.

But this was all about to change a little, I hoped, as I took a yellow and white maxi taxi from Deygo (Diego Martin) into *tong* (town/Port-of-Spain) to meet Gillian Goddard. *Finally*, I thought, the ancestors had heard my pleas for some guidance in a country that, with every sound and smell, seemed to recall the presence of my grandmother. But it was also as foreign to me as any place could be, and bouts of alienation seemed to pounce upon me at regular intervals, reminding me that I could never get too comfortable. "Both/and" is a duality I learned from Keiko Kubo, a Japanese-American activist in Oakland, and I try to exercise it as much as I can.

It is the first time I am going to venture into town alone since leaving Trinidad as a teenager. I receive ample warnings from my family — *Trinidad change*, they tell me, *it not the same.* Horror stories of brutal crimes are repeated like American news cycles. But I know that I have to break out of the crippling fear that seems to imprison so many, like the metal bars that are installed over windows to keep burglars out, only seeming to cage me in. Imagine, an island that sometimes could be as beautiful as paradise, where the inhabitants are afraid to leave their concrete homes. This is the reality for many there.

But not everyone. When I arrive, I see the car almost immediately, parked at the side of the road, across the street from the Savannah, that giant expanse of green that I once walked along on school days, from Belmont into *tong*. I find Gillian Goddard, waiting in a beaten-up sedan that will take us both to *the land*. Once I've made my way to the car, I see it is full of various items that show an enterprising spirit: gardening tools and gadgets that only a woman who uses her hands would ever need, a box full of empty mason jars, a pair of rubber boots. This is the first time that we are meeting in person, and I immediately feel at home in her presence. I slide into the passenger seat, feeling for the first time since I landed in Trinidad, some kind of ease. Today, we'll be driving about an hour away from Port-of-Spain into the mountains of St. Joseph, Maracas. Finally, I will see the land, which funnily enough is always hugging my vision, the vast expanse of the northern range always there, always holding me, always calling to me. Goddard's eyes are intense, her skin a golden brown. Her smile is open and warm like the sun that shines on most days here.

It's the first time I'm in Trinidad in over ten years, and I'm curious about what is happening in this twin-island nation. She seems to be a great person to ask. Historically, Trinidad and Tobago, like many of the other islands in the Caribbean, was once inhabited by the Indigenous of this region — the Caribs and the Arawaks. The end of their world would seem to occur with the arrival of the Spanish. Passed around like women in the patriarchy, the islands shifted between colonial European hands. It was Trinidad and Tobago's fate to be British subjects for extraction — from the forced labour of enslaved Africans and their descendants, to the rebranding of this system called "indentureship" under the recommendation of a sugar plantation owner in Guiana, John Gladstone, whose last name, ironically enough, my East Indian grandfather bore as his middle name.

In a way, the violence of plantation life can still be felt on the island, from what many perceive and interpret as a sort of lawlessness, the archaic prison that I walked past every day on Frederick Street, and, even as in my grandfather's case, the carrying of foreign names that seem as out-of-place here as an Enid Blyton book (which is still read here in this mostly Black country). Fast forward and Trinidad and Tobago develops a pretty robust economy thanks to another form of extraction: crude oil. Unlike so many other Caribbean nations, Trinidad and Tobago has managed to sustain a relatively large middle class. Upward mobility is available to some, usually among certain skin tones, although not exclusively so, and the overwhelmingly poor demographics seem to still be the descendants of enslaved Africans and indentured Indians. This country hasn't been buffered from many of the symptoms of late-stage capitalism, however, especially how it pertains to Black and Indigenous communities. As we drive by colourful street stands, and vast fields of green, with periods of traffic congestion, Gillian responds.

"I don't think you can separate our situation here in Trinidad from what's happening globally. Maybe there was a time in history that you could look at parts of the world and their situation might be much more different from each other. But it's not like that now." She goes on to tell me about the evidence that there have been people living in both Trinidad and Tobago for thousands of years. Goddard drives expertly through the congestion of traffic that a country that has more cars than people inadvertently produces. She tells me about the pottery she often finds on the land she and a collective of others are currently rehabilitating, and that the pieces are hundreds of years old. According to Goddard, these early inhabitants had probably moved up from South America, expanding into the Caribbean both permanently and temporarily. But the difference between them and us, Goddard maintains, is that "Indigenous people are not dumb. They developed thinking over hundreds of thousands of years. They had time to play and to figure it out. Then they make that into a culture. And there are certain behaviours that help that culture to be able to sustain itself in that land base and with neighbouring cultures. And so, people make decisions based on this. But right now, what we're doing is not culture-building." Part of this knowledge/culture they exercised, she says, was not keeping permanent, densely populated land base settlements.

FEEDBACK LOOPS

But, Goddard continues, this is something we are not practicing now. "These decisions that we make in our culture have absolutely nothing to do with the needs and limitations of our land base. We are making decision after decision in a vacuum and our feedback loop is coming from other humans living in civilization instead of the land which is such an absolutely unintelligent way to have a feedback loop."

And Goddard loves feedback loops. "I think about it all the time. If I do something, I want the feedback to come back to me really, really fast. I want to feel it. I don't drink, I don't smoke. I don't use things to stop feeling the feedback loop. I try to feel it. So, if I do something in the morning, I want to feel the flow of it, I want to feel if it's making sense."

Our bodies, Goddard says, are the most sophisticated

instruments that can be used to tune us into these feedback loops. "Our bodies give us information all the time, but you have to be in a state to hear it, to feel it. If there's too much going on or if we have had the skill of listening to our bodies overridden by authoritarian figures such as parents, teachers, political systems, cultural norms; then we start to lose our ability to tune into the intelligence of our own bodies. This is what schools do, for example. It teaches us to not listen to our own bodies…"

CIVILIZATION IS NOT SCIENCE-BASED

"You could call it what you want to call it, but it's not science. Science is something that actually looks at evidence and then makes conclusions based on evidence, of processes that are naturally happening." According to Goddard, the controlled processes that our culture does in the name of science, including treating animals horribly in order to obtain data, "is the most unsophisticated and short-sighted form of science that you could ever find. You go and you look at *terra preta* soil in the Amazon rainforest, and how the Indigenous population were able to grow things there by creating fertility, by making biochar in their soil with burnt pottery that allowed them to plant in infertile areas." They did this because the soil in the rainforest is not very fertile, so they created the conditions needed to support populations larger than those that could be supported by what was there naturally. Thousands of years later, says Goddard, the soil is still there, still fertile. Yet, she marvels, we look at them as lesser beings, lesser cultures, unsophisticated. "Just because you can't read a language doesn't mean the language isn't saying something, and that's fundamentally what it comes down to. That the people who had encounters with these groups, the people coming from Europe, were clueless. They didn't and still don't know how to interpret what's going on. They actually thought forests were untouched when they came to North America. But the forests were tightly collaborated with. We have to be careful of the world 'managed' because that's not really the way that culture operated."

For Goddard, this has so much to do with human supremacy. She admits that she, too, is a human supremacist — that no one can really escape it in the West. "The level of stupidity of ignoring feedback loops has gotten us to the point where we actually have a planet where our stupidity has now created global problems of instability of temperature and rainfall, when we actually got this thing that was working fairly well." She tells me about the people who once lived at the mouth of the Seattle River who didn't have to be nomadic because there was so much food there. "They were eating things that we go to the most expensive restaurants to eat. And they were there munching down on all kinds of seafood. Many, many groups were doing that all over the place." And if there was one thing the Europeans were right about, it is that in multiple documents from initial contact these people were described as "happy". That is certainly something to think about.

Goddard, who home-schooled both her children, is not just about articulating what many would term controversial ideas. And if you're the type to think of home-schooling as a dirty word, her oldest is faring quite well at a prestigious East Coast university. Goddard gets her hands, literally, in the dirt. Take, for example, the land that we're on our way to see. A large part of the project is to re-establish the earth, to return it to its quality before the human cultivation of crops stripped it of its fertility. While there, I help her shovel the biochar that she and her community are in the process of producing so that it can be used to revitalise the earth.

Goddard returns to the subject of the consequences of losing the ability to use our bodies as the sophisticated instruments that they are built to be. "So, after a while, you stop knowing what nonsense sounds like, whether somebody is appropriate to be around, whether they are making good decisions, whether your body needs more food in it, whether it's time to go to the bathroom, whether you're feeling some sort of sexual desire, whether the weather means you have to move to another place. *Our bodies are no longer available as an instrument.* There is no instrument that we can have access to that is as sensitive, and full of ability to take in information, measure it, and give you the results, the feedback loop, as our body. It's made for that. It's sophisticated." She goes on to say that our bodies are not binoculars, not a hearing aid, or even a temperature sensor. "It's all of these things and more. We have those abilities inside of our body." But when we have lost the skill to use our bodies in this way, "you're making decisions based on 'are you going to get a raise? Are you going to get in trouble? Is somebody going to like you?' Those are all different ways to make decisions and those are not necessarily the best way. In that sense, *the whole system is set up for us to ignore our bodies."*

Goddard has a chocolate company that offers support to communities to (re)learn the art of chocolate making, whilst Goddard and her crew also support them to have their own businesses. Building local economies is something that Goddard takes very seriously, and she is quick to remind me that it was in the markets in Africa that our foremothers traded in future markets, way before Wall Street was even conceived. "I love how capitalism has failed here in Trinidad," she tells me, as she drives the car effortlessly through the bacchanalian city traffic. "It's failure has forced us to have actual relationships with each other just for survival." She goes on to explain that she rarely ever buys anything directly other than food. "That's why I love living in what they call the 'Third World'. We have an elaborate and inclusive way of doing business."

There is something about the decaying vibe of Port-of-Spain that I find to be an honest reflection of the global economy. I've been traveling for a few months at this point, throughout the US mostly, and one of the things I noticed almost immediately was the vast volume of businesses being shuttered, even before the pandemic. There is something about the general neglect of Port-of-Spain, the souls left to wander and live on the streets, that says everything that we need to know about how colonisation continues to leave its mark on this island.

Goddard has also been passionately involved in organising local organic farmers to deliver fresh, organic and plastic-free food products to customers. When she realised that the challenge wasn't only about making chocolate, but getting it to market, "We founded a group, which we call an NGO. We now have about ten communities collaborating throughout the Caribbean region, called the Alliance of Rural Communities. In Trinidad we offer a local organic produce box that we sell a couple of times a month." Her projects include revitalising trades like cocoa farming and processing in rural villages throughout the Caribbean and ensuring that skills that were once lost are being used towards the benefit of the villagers, as opposed to their exploitation.

Her chocolate company is called Sun Eaters, which she says is a reference to the fact that everything we eat comes from the sun's energy. Goddard's foray into chocolate-making was not something she had planned. In fact, she says, it happened by accident. At the time, she and her partner were drying bananas to help a friend when she realised that Trinidad had been importing all of its cocoa products, including cocoa nibs. This was surprising for her to learn, especially since Trinidad was once home to multiple cocoa plantations. Seeing an opportunity, Goddard taught herself how to make cocoa nibs in order to supply the market. And since she now had nibs, it seemed natural to progress into making chocolate. This all happened, she says, within a six-month period. Once she started making chocolate, she and her partner realised how crazy the situation actually was.

The car has come to a stop at a busy intersection. There are street vendors hawking various wares — oranges that are green; newspapers with violent headlines; mangoes cut up in plastic bags (*chow*). The sun is at the apex of its heat and I am thankful that we at least have the benefit of the passing breeze when the car is in motion. Goddard beckons to a young lady who is selling oranges. She looks young, a teenager still, her posture tells the story of a dignity that cannot be stifled. Goddard exchanges some pleasantries as well as some brightly coloured bills for a bag of oranges. As the girl smiles in gratitude and makes her way back amongst the traffic, Goddard continues, "Can you imagine every day, having to come out here in the hot sun to try and scrape together some money? And her whole family is probably depending on her for that." Goddard has a look in her eyes that seem to be smouldering with passion, which matches the way in which she sees things. The poor are not invisible to her, as they seem to be for so many others. "Our culture has a very abusive relationship to how we treat our poor," she concludes, not unreasonably.

Back in the car, she continues to tell me the story of how she got into chocolate. "We thought that our friends who are farmers should be making chocolate instead of selling beans." Realising that it was now a "lost knowledge", she and her partner set out to teach others how to make chocolate. That was about four and a half years ago. All of this is perhaps why she confesses to me that she feels she is not a very focused person. But I have to disagree. I see the myriad projects and interests that she's involved in as being very focused on the process of restoring balance to what the West has labelled the "ecosystem", but which is the ancient, delicate and sacred relationship we have and have had with our Earth; the one that has been so violated by colonialism, capitalism and corporatization.

"A lot of my interest is in non-human forms of life and being an ally as a human. Right now, we're in a situation where this thing we call civilization, which we think is such a beautiful and wonderful thing, that is so full of such great achievements, is actually destroying our planet. We have not paid attention to the price of civilization. We haven't paid attention to the feedback loop. For me, in my internal language, which is the only one I could understand, I have a contrast between Indigeneity, which is rooted in your land-base, and civilization which is rooted in dense human communities."

Goddard explains that over the years she's read and explored on her own this idea of civilization and she's discovered a pattern. "I've seen that these dense human communities are things that intelligent indigenous cultures would often have for short periods of time. The waste that a dense community produces and the needs that it has, for food, shelter, materials, are almost impossible to sustain over long periods of time." In this way, she explains, a group might spend some time together, in a particular geographical space, for maximum a couple of hundred years. "Tops. But this ongoing idea, that we in the West have, that you could actually live for centuries in these dense communities where you're growing nothing, you're not providing your own water, you're doing all these other things that somebody else has to do for you and the land base has to do for you."

Her words seem particularly haunting to me now, as 2007 was the year that the UN estimated that, for the first time in history, there are more people living in urban areas than rural.

"This idea is so arrogant, that we actually think that we can live in dense communities for hundreds of years. Have operas and cathedrals and all of these things..." She shakes her head in disbelief as the car is on an incline and makes its way up through the bush and up the hills.

The more Goddard read the more she realised that our ancestors knew much more than we do when it came to community and culture-building. "They would settle in different areas for periods of time and then move on. But this thing that we're doing on and on and on and now we're, like, addicted to it. We think that this is actually a rational way to live." And this of course has consequences. "People who don't have as much power are forced to go places," like into cities, which further exacerbates the imbalance. "And now, we're trying to build machines to replace the people in rural communities so we could keep extracting."

It's hard to believe that Gillian Goddard was on her way to leaving Trinidad, like so many others who are offered a way out. Like so many of us, she had found herself running from the very origin of her existence, to be a woman, to be Black and to be poor. "I had kind of convinced myself that I was middle-class. I screened out the things that contradicted that. That's what we do here. We don't look at the things, or don't include them in our lives, that contradict this thing that we don't want to be. And we only include the things that prove our point of who we are (or who we believe ourselves to be.) I had done that for a long time. I was in elite schools; I was around people who had more privilege."

Until one day, when she was in the middle of a counselling session at her university and the counsellor looked at her and asked, "But you don't have very much, do you? And that was the beginning of a very big tailspin. Clearly, I had not convinced people, at least this person, as much as I thought I had. When I realised that my education was taking me away from where I came from, that's when I turned all my efforts to learning how I could best assist in strengthening poor, vulnerable Black women. My mother was poor and Black, her mother was poor and Black. This is my lineage and I own it." She realised that, although she had been given privilege, she was not going to turn her back and walk away from her own community. She made a conscious decision to take her skills back to where she came from. It has not always been easy, Goddard admits.

"We convince ourselves that we are something other than our historical foundation. That was a very pivotal step for me in really coming back home, class wise. Not denying the fact that I had been given so-called privilege because of skin colour, hair texture, but being very clear who is my group. So, when I'm doing something, I'm not doing something *to* or *for* poor people, or *to* poor communities, even though I have taken on the accent and sometimes the posture of people with privilege. I'm very, very clear, that this is my community. This is who my people are. That was important."

Finally, we arrive at the top of the mountain. When we get out of the car, the vast expanse of green that is below us is mesmerising. We passed a few houses on our way here, but it is far from being as congested as it tends to be in the city. There are trees and plants all around us, and as I take in the cool of the bush, Goddard reminds me, "Imagine, the whole of Trinidad used to be like this".

"The thing is, even the people within my working-class community were rooting for me to get out, so after I started shifting back, it was very traumatic for people, my family members, or other people who saw getting out as your salvation. So, it wasn't like people felt there was a choice, right? Like if you're given the opportunity, to escape from this powerless situation of oppression, you should take it. And I remember once talking to some relatives about it." She had confronted them that they hadn't known what they had to give up for the newfound material wealth to be found through migrating to the States or wherever else opportunity seemed to beckon. "This is not a trade-off for nothing, all these myths, right, stories and religious books, about being given money, like the devil giving you money, that's how I felt it was. You're getting wealth and privilege, but you were losing something. So now, the thing is I have seen the range. I have been in situations where I have seen some of the wealthiest people in the world and I have been in some really financially deprived situations. So, I know it's not this privileged life that you move to and suddenly it's like all peaches. There are a lot of horrible things there, horrible values of selfishness and egotism. There is a lot of denial of your own humanity in order to survive in those worlds, and I'm just not prepared to do it. It's not a trade-off for me at all at this point." Goddard goes on to encourage me to look at how the most wealthy treat their children. "They send their children away — can you imagine what type of human beings that creates? That your parents don't even want you around?!"

Through Gillian Goddard, I was able to meet *the land* — learn a bit about the possibilities for not only Trinidad and Tobago, but the entire planet. During my visit, students from secondary schools were taking to the streets, joining the global movement of children protesting the state of the environment, thanks to a civilization that, as Goddard would put it, has grown either unable or unwilling to listen to feedback loops. "We need new systems," she tells me, as we take turns, turning the glowing coconut husks in very much the same way people who first came from South America perhaps once did in order to revitalize the land.

While I was in Trinidad there was an influx of Venezuelans, fleeing god only knows, not too far from our shores. The tone in which they were written about, spoken about was horrifying. Especially if one is to consider that there has been movement between what we call "Venezuela" and "Trinidad" (and the rest of the islands for that matter) for ever. At the time, many Venezuelans at the detention centre were on a hunger strike to protest the conditions they were forced to live in. It was sombre reminder that it is not only white supremacy that is our enemy, but that there is something darker at play — and again, Goddard was helpful in helping me understand and even articulate this dynamic. "I like to use words like 'oppressor role' — it's the role of a person who has the power in that interaction, or situation, and who also has power in the same system, so that they can get away with it."

Goddard says that in her "change work", i.e., the work that she has to personally engage in to be that difference, she finds it "extremely useful to notice where I take on the oppressor role. Whether it's giving people the support needed to not be afraid of money — which is something you'll often find in communities where the money is tight. Or giving people support in collaborating with each other, where, in a place with the plantation history we have here, of really heavy oppression, people were taught to rat on each other. So, it's really hard for people to collaborate. Through all of that type of work, I found that it's really helpful for me to look at how I behave in an oppressor role and to understand that."

Goddard uses the example of her children to drive her point home. "I have two children living in my house, and I behave oppressively towards them in individual ways and in systemic ways. I think understanding how oppressors behave, it's helped me to notice how hard it is to view yourself as an oppressor. How intertwined it is to a victim role. That being called out as an oppressor, as the person who is abusing power, there is also an automatic response of victim feeling. So, when my children call me out for talking to them in a certain tone of voice or choosing to live in a certain place where they don't want to live, or not distributing enough money in the household, I feel hurt. I feel like I'm the victim. This helped me when I'm confronting people, when I'm saying to them, 'hey, you're behaving patriarchal, or you're behaving like a white racist', that I know that the first response from them is going to be the feeling that they are being blamed, victimized. 'I'm a victim', we think, because that's what I do, when somebody calls me out for it, that's my first reaction."

Goddard shares with me her ideas about parenting, which I find refreshing. She says that the way we parent in our culture is to train our children to live in an oppressive society. "That's the current world. The whole way that young people are brought up is really horrible. But we love our children. Now often when we can feel the love, which is always so funny to me, is when they're sleeping. We look at them asleep and we feel such an outpouring of love for them. When they are not being children. We also love our parents after they're dead. We absolutely love that. But we can't handle them in real life. That's fundamentally a big piece of what it comes down to. We, as civilization, are being taught to actually be necrophiliacs — that's the word that I've been using. We like our chair, but we don't like the tree. We choose the dead form over the living."

"One of the groups that I learn a lot from about my activism is the Sami. They're supposed to be white, but they're treated like crap. It's not just about whiteness, it's about Indigeneity and biophilia — there's a hatred of biophilic culture. If a culture is close to life, and is close to the rhythms of life, and treats life, learning, and animals, with respect, and moves around and is not tied into institutions, the land base, then we treat them badly. Currently, the Sami are being persecuted horribly, and the rate of suicide in the Sami communities is incredibly high."

"When we say European, let's talk about *civilized* Europeans. Let's not lump the indigenous European, rare as they are, in the sentence. I feel the same way about humans. People say humans are like that; no, *civilized* humans are like that. This is not saying that Indigenous humans are to be worshipped like if there is no challenge in the way that they're organized. But if you're studying Indigenous people, please don't give me any data about Indigenous people who have been contacted by civilization in any intense way. Those are amongst the most traumatized populations in the world, the loss of their biophilic culture and how these necrophiliacs are acting so insanely that they almost go mentally ill."

In the end, however, Goddard is optimistic. I asked her

about *Afro-optimism* — a word I had been playing around with for some time to counter "Afropessimism". "I'm an optimist at heart, and some of that is growing up from a history of poverty, historical poverty. People survived, and they found ways to make it, so there must be some optimism that's maybe even inherited. We keep expecting that we're going to make it, or we keep trying to make it. I think that I trust DNA, and I trust life. Climate change is a feedback loop, so we're actually getting a chance to check ourselves. If I were to say I had a religion, I would say it's the religion of feedback loops. Imagine we are so lucky to have feedback loops. Could you imagine if you just do things and you never get any feedback? You would have no clue. So, strengthening feedback loops is really useful. Let's give people the ability to really strengthen and act based on feedback loops."

KEN WEAVING / GRACE BLAKELEY

For most of my life, if you had asked me who my hero was, I would have said my grandfather, Ken Weaving. That is, as long as my extremely loving but competitive grandma, Doreen, wasn't in earshot. My grandad, as we called him, died when I was fourteen. Grandma is still here, but she recently had a stroke so she's probably not going to get around to reading this essay.

Grandad was born in London and was, by all accounts, a difficult child. My mother, when reflecting on my own misbehaviour, would tell me how he had been sent to borstal — a word with which I wasn't familiar, but which summoned up Dickensian images of waifs being locked in dank cupboards. My parents often joked about how they might develop their own contained space for me — my godfather suggested boarding school in Scotland, but my parents promptly informed him that I would find a way to escape.

Eventually, grandad decided — at the ripe age of fourteen — to leave home and join the merchant navy. This was another phrase with which I wasn't familiar, and for a long time I assumed that it was just a subsection of the navy — until I met someone who had actually been in the navy, proudly telling him about my grandad, only to be informed that the merchant navy doesn't actually have much to do with the Royal Navy at all. This probably explains why my grandfather left England at fourteen a staunch monarchist and returned a republican — and a communist.

When he came back to London, he met my grandma — who loves to tell us that at the time she was referred to as "the Queen of Ladbroke Grove". She had been one of eleven children raised in what my mother — always trying to boost her working-class credentials — referred to as a "slum". Yet somehow my great grandmother lived to 102 — I still remember her 100th birthday at a civic centre in Notting Hill. She insisted on having a picture with me, my mum, her and her mother to show off the Oliver women of four generations — grandma was never particularly fond of her mother, but she did find solace in her longevity.

Most of my great-grandmother's eleven children were evacuated during the war. Grandma ended up in Trowbridge with a nice middle-class family, attended grammar school and returned to Ladbroke Grove with ideas far above her station. Hence the nickname. Though she likes to think it's because all the boys were in love with her. While working as a secretary — a substantial bit of social mobility for the time — she met my grandad. They married, had children and moved out of west London when — to quote Doreen — "all the West Indians moved in". Grandma voted Leave.

Grandad started working in logistics for Sainsbury's in Basingstoke — a job he would have for the rest of his life. He also joined the Transport and General Workers' Union, eventually becoming a shop steward. My mother, herself a lapsed anarcho-communist, proudly tells me that he was one of the first Westerners to visit the USSR as a tourist. I'll never forget coming home from a history lesson in which we'd been learning about the horrors of Stalinism, only to be informed by Grandad that we'd all be living under Nazi rule were it not for the USSR.

Grandad didn't much take to trade unionism. He resented

all the perks he was offered as a shop steward, and frequently complained that the union brass was insufficiently militant. Mum says he could have risen up the ranks but chose not to. He became increasingly cynical about socialism over the course of his life, though he never let me know that. At one point I thought a great way to impress him would be to get a tattoo (he had a lot of tattoos) of the anarcho-communist insignia — an anarchy sign in which a sickle slices through the line in the middle of the "A", and the right side of the "A" is a hammer. After he died, when I was fourteen, I chose to get some stars on my wrist instead.

I thought my grandad was the coolest person in the world — a vision I now realise I inherited directly from my mother. I think he saw a lot of himself in me too. Just before he died, I had a letter published in the *New Statesman* in response to an article about Gordon Brown replacing Blair as PM. I think I had written about how Brown would represent a step forward from the misguided hopes and betrayals of the Blair years — something it would be quite natural for a fourteen-year-old girl to have believed. Grandad bought a copy and had it framed.

He had a similar level of pride in — and similarly high expectations for — my mother. Mum became the golden child by escaping her comprehensive school and jetting off to Cambridge — a fact that, in our warped class system, allows her to continue to refer to herself as working-class. When she arrived at Fitzwilliam College as part of the first cohort of female students ever to attend the college, she reports being mistaken for a Russian princess — partly because she was quiet and beautiful with a penchant for faux fur, but partly because none of the other undergraduates recognised her from school.

For most of the rest of her life, mum carried around the weight of being the upwardly mobile daughter of a communist. She and my father — who met as undergraduates at Fitz — travelled around the world after university and, ever keen to support the socialist cause, travelled to Nicaragua to "pick coffee beans for the revolution", only to find that picking coffee beans is a very sensitive process and one for which their indelicate fingers were poorly equipped.

After a few years of travelling, my mum came back to the UK and decided to get a job in the post-Big Bang City of London. It was her naïve belief that if she could infiltrate the UK's financial system, she would eventually reach a position in which she would be able to support demands for a debt jubilee to the Third World. Instead, she ended up working on the trading floor of Barclay's. After a few twists and turns, she decided to do a PhD, which she completed while raising two young children. Dr Karen Blakeley then turned her PhD into a book, before putting work on the backburner to care for a daughter, who insisted upon continuously getting expelled from school.

For most of my life, if you had asked me who my hero was, I would have said my grandfather, as long as my grandmother wasn't in earshot. He is, after all, the man who gave me my politics. I wrote about him in the personal statement that got me into Oxford. But then I think about my mother, who is still struggling to figure out who she is after spending her life feeling as though she was the type of person who might save the world — a projection of my grandad, who always wanted to be such a person, but never was.

Then I think about my own journey: the confidence I have from attending private school and Oxford, and from constantly being loved and reinforced by my parents. But also, the nagging sense that if I didn't *do* something to justify that privilege, then I may as well never have been born. I think about how painful it must have been for my mother to carry the weight of those expectations around with her for her entire life, only subconsciously to pass them on to me, and watch me transform them into reality.

Perhaps on its own, that realisation would be nothing more than a little sad. But my mother hasn't allowed this to be the end of her story. A few years ago, she travelled to the US for a shamanistic spiritual retreat deep in the Colorado desert, where she informs me that she found her spirit animal and came face to face with the demons from her past. A year later, she signed up for another retreat — this time, one in which she would take ayahuasca and spend the entire evening vomiting while staring into the depths of her own soul. A year after that, to the utter shock of everyone we knew, she left my father. They had been, by all accounts, the perfect couple — but she didn't want to live as one half of someone else's story anymore. She wanted to figure out who she was. She's still on that journey, as is my incredible dad, and I'm right there with both of them.

For most of my life, if you had asked me who my hero was, I would have said my grandfather, as long as my grandmother wasn't in earshot. He was bold, intelligent and militant. He was strident and unshakable in his beliefs. He taught me how to be a socialist. But today, if you ask me who my hero is, I can't think of anyone other than my mother.

Mum, like most women, including my grandma, has spent her whole life carrying around her own and other people's pain. The pain of other people's dashed expectations, and the pain of failing to live up to those expectations herself. The pain of other people's loss, oppression and exploitation, and the pain of knowing she could never do anything to stop it. The pain of experiencing a constant nagging sense that her life shouldn't feel this way; that there was something more out there for her, but something that would always remain unreachable.

But my mum, unlike most women, including my grandma, decided — at the tender age of 62 — to do something about it. She looked at her life — stable, happy, nice — and realised that there had to be something more. She started with tarot reading and hallucinogenic drugs, but she has set out on a journey that could take her anywhere. This is not the journey of Nietzsche's superman, heroically casting off the shackles of religion and morality to realise his place in the pantheon of the gods; and it is certainly not the journey of Ayn Rand's rugged individualist, desperate to escape the constraints imposed on him by the oppressive normality of social life. It is the journey of someone trying authentically to discover what it really means to be free.

My grandad may have given me my politics but seeing my mother's struggle has reaffirmed to me why I remain a socialist. She is lucky enough to have the resources — financial, emotional and intellectual — she needs to start this journey. But under capitalism most people aren't so lucky, especially not women. A woman without my mother's pension would never have been able to leave my father at this stage in her life — she would, like many women, be stuck in a fine but unfulfilling relationship simply because she couldn't afford to live alone.

Socialists imagine a world in which we all have everything we need to live our best and fullest lives. A world in which our creativity isn't constrained by work; our sexuality isn't constrained by a mortgage; and our curiosity isn't constrained by economic insecurity. To me, socialism is a world in which every slightly-less-than-happy 62-year-old woman can go on a life-altering journey of self-discovery without worrying about being able to survive when it's over.

Mark at Bawdsey, Suffolk, April 2011.

MARK FISHER / ANDY SHARP

In his book *The Dream and the Underworld,* James Hillman discusses two placements of the hero. One is as the Herculean ego, very much our standard perception today, operating in the glare of the daylight. The second is the idea of the hero dwelling in the underworld, bound to tragedy, and remembered by monuments to their struggles with the vicissitudes of life. Accepting that Mark's untimely and awful death positions him as the latter, it therefore seems right to celebrate two lasting qualities of his personality.

INCLUSIVITY

This was at the heart of Mark's sensibility, and from my first contact, via e-mail, to our first meeting, it was obvious that he was keen to include me in both his social circle and his cultural project. We met in 2006, shortly after he moved to Suffolk for the first time, connecting on the back of a shared love for the eerie geography of M.R. James. It was fascinating to see someone drawn to other shapes along the estuaries. One particular photo entry in his blog stood out, documenting the rotting carcasses of old boats on the banks near Woodbridge. Though I had been in Suffolk a decade, I had never "seen" them as Mark had. We were on the same wavelength but wore different binoculars. I was invited to dinner; hospitalities were reciprocated and we began to socialise.

Mark joined the Bawdsey Radar Group, and I took my family along to their open day, where Mark was broadcasting a sound piece in one of the units. Here was a different configuration of Mark's comfort with inclusivity, gaining confidence with enthusiasts and former staff at the base. He'd later incorporate their fascinating archive into *On Vanishing Land*. There was nothing ironic or arch about his interest in Bawdsey, certainly no public service broadcast, but part of a personal dive into local history and a desire to recognise unsung heroes of World War II — it was mostly women who were stationed at the radar base. There was clear mutual respect between Mark and the group.

Late in 2007, Mark asked to me speak at his "Weird Symposium" at Goldsmiths. Though I was not academically affiliated, I think it was a testament to Mark's inclusivity that I felt entirely welcome and appreciated. I also met half a dozen or so people who became good friends, and I think that Mark's injection of inclusivity was a vital fuel for those on an autodidactic path.

But I think this nurturing generosity was a broader concern of Mark's that created a space for free-ranging conversation, both on his blog and in person: a democracy of subject matter that was key to dismantling snobbery. At its simplest, being able to discuss art and sport with equal gravity. It's possible for philosophy to apply to all areas of the playing pitch. This inclusivity of interest makes it so much easier to swap ideas, and find unexpected, shared fascinations. On one occasion, over at my place, Mark spotted a copy of Judy and Fred Vermorel's *Starlust* on the bookshelf and asked to borrow it to discuss with some students. Again, inclusivity here reveals itself as a willingness to pull in vagrant strains of culture and treat them as vital raw material for a new anthropology.

SENSITIVITY

Revisiting the *k-punk* blog today is a disconcerting experience, because the writing is so incandescent, the narrative hypnotically organic and the voice still discernible. Within a few paragraphs, you begin to read it in *his* voice. These blog entries were very much "routines", similar in a way to the letters of William Burroughs that became *The Naked Lunch*. However, I also had the pleasure of working with Mark on a few projects where he revealed remarkable sensitivity as an audio-visual conceptualist and communicator. In 2013, Mark and Justin Barton offered me the opportunity to help produce the visual component for their *On Vanishing Land* show and to engineer his field recordings for interludes in the soundtrack of the main essay. These became interspersed between the curated pieces by the likes of Raime, Gazelle Twin and Ekoplekz.

To gather sounds and images, Mark and I revisited the locations he and Justin had walked and written about: Bawdsey, Sutton Hoo and Felixstowe Port. It was near sunset when we walked around Landguard Peninsula, where the fort decays into World War II watch towers. A Ballardian landscape that Mark seemed inexorably drawn toward. The port here is a creaking, slow-moving, endless procession of mega-capitalism, and as we tried to steer the microphone to capture and isolate all these sounds, Mark noted something to the effect of, "I was thinking, if only we had the apparatus to really pick this up, but we have… it's our ears".

It's a comment that I think about often. It's obviously typical Mark, witty and lucid, but also a recognition that the human is the most sensitively attuned organism — all technology flounders to achieve our perception.

When we came to put together the video collage for *On Vanishing Land,* Mark's direction was to continually lower the sound signal, until it was almost imperceptible. Similarly, for the slide sequence, we devised an achingly slow fade to and from white, between the images, stretching the transitions ever more at Mark's request. As we did so, we both started to see almost phantom white negatives of the preceding and emerging images in the sequence. I think this reflected Mark's desire to invoke a kind of hallucinatory absence and an interest in technology as the subtlest touch or even some filter to hollow out brash realities and evolve an ambient epiphany. I also recall him playing a penny whistle into one of the concrete vents at Bawdsey, in homage to M.R James, a recording that we stretched into a long, siren cry, one that delighted him; both eerie and therapeutic. I look back and think there was a psychological aspect to these creative directives, that reality might have been emotionally overwhelming for Mark, as a result of however the internal apparatus of senses are calibrated. What I thought was a striving for an aesthetic effect was also a desire to quieten down the world. To listen to the silence. Depression might have its root in a damping and protective mechanism, but the ensuing silence has an awful tendency to turn on itself. The inner critic becomes the dark siren of depression.

Amidst the many and justified eulogies, I think these two qualities — his innate sensitivity and his inclusivity — were attributes, bravely worn, in the hyper-connected world.

They might have not been the steel shields needed as one cuts their way through an increasingly combative public sphere, but they are attributes that continue to inspire, involve and raise consciousness.

PETER BARNES / TARIQ GODDARD

My very early days were not particularly bookish; books would come, but they would arrive later. My father drilled me in martial values and a form of stoical machismo that I still have a wary regard for, my mother with an earnest belief in God, which also still persists, and I credit them both for making me roughly as they intended me to be. Neither of them thought they were selling me abstractions, and although they both expressed some difficulty in understanding who I was, they did everything they could for me given the people they were, and there is nothing I hold against them or myself regarding the outcome.

It was our good friend and neighbour Peter Barnes, however, my "Uncle" Peter, who had the greatest influence in what I was to specifically do with my life. He offered me the noblest, most uncompromising and deliberately unworldly advice imaginable, which at the time may have appeared slightly less bizarre than it does now, which nonetheless set me on my path as a writer. His example encouraged me to begin, and then continue writing, which despite the inevitable ebbs and flows in popularity, to say little of the hostility, warmth and indifference with which my work has been received, helped me persist with my vocation, novel after novel, to a point where writing a book and finishing became the way I divided up life. Moreover, he provided me with the ground-zero punk rock attitude that has undoubtedly harmed my "career"; at the same time as ensuring that I have the self-respect necessary to write and create fiction and survive in an industry that does not always esteem its writers.

I grew up in what I now recognise was a bohemian milieu, right in the centre of London amongst people on their way up and way down. That we were all allowed to live so close to the capital's landmarks at all, in light of the gentrification and economic cleansing that followed, seems in itself to have been a small historical miracle. Our neighbours were people who wanted to hide away from the judgment of society, some were dissolute hedonists, others mixed race or gay couples cohabiting, the odd politician in exile, and scores of people who worked round the theatre: actors, stagehands, carpenters, prop makers, chauffeurs, the lady that pulled the curtains at the National, and Peter Barnes, a successful playwright who nonetheless comported himself with genial grace and mocking self-deprecation. Indeed, years after he died an acquaintance known to us both told me he had always assumed that Peter lectured at some polytechnic or other, until he watched Alan Rickman read the address at his funeral and was persuaded otherwise.

Peter and his first wife Charlotte were very close to my parents, despite having nothing in common with them, apart from living three doors down, and I grew up calling Peter Uncle, while he named me Sunny Jim, as I was an optimistic baby and hopeful small boy. On my first day of school, he gave me a book on Joan of Arc which he correctly guessed would amuse my father, taught me to play chess before I could spell it, and read me all of the Sherlock Holmes stories, that he regularly improved upon and embellished. Unusually for the time, Peter owned his own small Mews house, which he had bought with the proceeds to his first hit, *The Ruling Class* — an unnecessary extravagance, everyone said, until the Church Commissioners began evicting all their protected tenants some years some years later, my family included.

Peter was to the left of the Labour Party, which my parents thought was actually funny, as did others in a community that was cheerfully and broadly tolerant without being explicitly political: a shy stage builder affiliated to the WRP[1] was the other exception. My mother and father, who were invited to Peter's first nights, considered his plays insane, regarding his oeuvre with merry disbelief, yet they were proud that academics wrote books about him — even though they thought academics were insane too, along with anyone else who went into further education. Although Peter played down his acclaim locally, as I grew up, I discovered he was iconoclastic, and when pushed, believed his plays were funnier than Shakespeare, better constructed than those of his more successful contemporaries and worthy of even more acclaim than they received. Despite his lightly worn erudition and learning, he had a coarse vitality, acquired perhaps from the seaside amusements his parents ran in Clacton, and was not afraid to directly confront people or states of affairs he did not like volubly, be that the anti-social behaviour of neighbours, the opinions of other playwrights who were essentially "journalists", or the changing governments of the day. Though I did not want to be a writer *because* of him, I did want to be *like* him, and watching Peter gave me my model for what a genuine

---

1 The WRP, The Workers Revolutionary Party, were a Trotskyist organisation with a largish following in theatrical circles at the time, mainly thanks to the unwavering support of Vanessa and Colin Redgrave.

writer should be, despite his doing nothing to encourage me to *actually* write (for that I have my beloved English teacher, John Stubbs, to thank, but that is another story).

In fact, Peter was capable of quite the reverse. He politely ignored my first literary efforts, doing no more than saying he had read them. He smiled at the first draft of my novel that I ran past him, and when I tried to obtain feedback, he would tell me that if I was writer I would get on and write whatever he or anyone else had to say, which is why there was no need for him to say anything. He blamed his silence on never having time to read, because of all the manuscripts he was sent, yet his recommendations for what *I* should read, and the pleasure he took in listening to my impressions thereof, counted as genuine, albeit indirect, encouragement. From my early teens he was damning about the actual life of a writer, and did not hold back, warning me of the frustration, humiliation and disappointment to come if I was to stick at it. Was it reverse psychology? It is hard to say, and to this day I am not sure, but looking back his exhortations that agents were not to be trusted, publishers did not trust their own judgement, critics were chancers and fakes, all seem like the sincere and practical advice to one who might follow in his footsteps. My instinct was to treat these horror stories as a secret code for the truly initiated, a test one had to pass, before earning the accolade of "writer".

As any writer knows, one's problems really start to come into their own after publication, and remaining in contention year in year out can be as difficult as gaining recognition in the first place, if not harder. As a publisher now, I know that much of the advice Peter gave me would mean career death were I to give it to my own writers, yet I would still respect any of them that followed it: say no to everything, be grave and do not be trivial, have nothing to do with publicity or self-promotion or literary celebrity of any kind; just write. While I did not follow this to the letter, certainly not as closely as Peter himself did, I believe I still adhered to it closely enough to take the least advantage of the opportunities then open to me. Peter believed real writers should only create, think and obsess about their work, so journalism was out, as was any kind of side-line that being a novelist might have given me a slight advantage in within media. As a real writer should not read reviews and certainly should not write them, far less teach creative writing or suck up to the industry in any way, my prospects lay entirely in my novels generating enough income to support me. Happily, they did, to start with. But were I to have continued to follow Peter's example into middle age, I would have become the J.D. Salinger of Paddington and struggled to feed myself, far less my family. Peter's views were simply too ungiving and hardcore to continue to cultivate into my thirties and beyond. Yet in an age where writers were already being encouraged to dilute the focus of their work by considering themselves cultural commemorators, with an opinion on everything from *Star Wars* to continental breakfasts, Peter showed me the true value of taking yourself seriously, even if other people laughed at you, or as likely, did not care who you were because their game was not yours.

Although I was only indirectly aware of it when growing up, following his own advice was sometimes a heavy burden for Peter too. He remained unclubbable, and despite being a favourite of actors from Peter O'Toole to Sean Connery, he was often out of the arts pages for years at a time. He paid a price for never being one of those names that are asked for their Summer Reading lists, sat at Hay next to the Clintons, or who find themselves on the mast head of the *LRB* and in the *ES* diary every fortnight. His early successes led to fallow periods when he lived a long way inside himself, his use of large casts making his plays difficult to stage, and despite his Oscar-nominated screenplays, acclaimed work on radio and late re-acclaim, he remained a self-condemned outsider to the end. Never being performative or contrived enough to have a tag placed on him meant that Peter was always hard to summarise, which in the long run can be lethal for a writer. Nothing gave him greater pleasure when, with my characteristic tactlessness, I told him people might assume he was dead, something he often repeated, proudly, as listeners squirmed in a discomfort he did not share.

Despite his formidable and mercurial first wife's descent into mental illness and his subsequent depression, Peter remarried happily and fulfilled his ambition to have children in his late sixties, first one and then triplets. He hoped he would be fit enough to play ping-pong with them in their teens, if not football, though sadly both speculations turned out to be too hopeful. He did live to see me get into print, and was tickled that my first novel's reception was so positive. The second novel was a "writer's" book, he said, which he enjoyed far more (there is probably more of him in it) and as I had locked into a style early on, he suggested I be more careless in the writing of my third, which he was not alive to see published, or any of the others which followed.

But by then I had learnt from him that everything is worth doing only for its own sake, there is no thanks, we are not part of a great plan, there is no justifying agenda, there is often little or no recognition for merit, and the only reward for staying the course is the respect of a few like-minded people, which is worth everything. This may be too harsh and desolate a philosophy for many, but as Peter had a religious belief in the value of his own writing and of writing in general, it was enough to inspire him to "respond to the whistle" every morning, writing in the British Library Reading Room, and after it was moved to Kings Cross, in the McDonalds at Marble Arch. One of the greatest compliments he paid me was how much he enjoyed our chats, especially the long ones in the park or stood outside our doorways, where he would laugh raucously as we employed Henry James and Joseph Conrad to disentangle the secrets of the universe, and where he would defer to my literary judgements. At such times I knew I had arrived and that these conversations were all the reward a writer's life required.

Since then, I have come to realise that I owe much of my intellectual self-confidence to Peter. In time this would mean I could work, edit and publish writers cleverer and with more academic qualifications than myself, having ruled out any other accommodation with the culture industry, and become a publisher. While I tend not to look up to people these days, any more than I would think of looking down on them, I grew up needing an example of who I could become, before I knew who I was, and Peter, who would have laughed if I picked Lee Marvin (who he considered a kindred spirt) instead of him, provided me with the rules, values and framework I recognise every time I raise my voice or shake my head. And for that, he will always be my hero.

CONTRIBUTORS

MARCUS BARNETT is the associate editor of *Tribune*.

GRACE BLAKELEY is a staff writer at *Tribune* and author of *Stolen: How to Save the World from Financialisation* and *The Corona Crash: How the Pandemic Will Change Capitalism*.

LESLEY-ANN BROWN is an American-born writer. She is the author of *Decolonial Daughter* and *Blackgirl on Mars*.

RYANN DONNELLY is an artist and academic. She is the author of *Justify My Love: Sex, Subversion, and Music Video*.

PETER FLEMING is a professor in Sydney, Australia. He is author of *The Worst is Yet To Come* and *Dark Academia: How Universities Die*.

TARIQ GODDARD is the author of seven novels and the publisher of Repeater Books.

GRAHAM HARMAN is Distinguished Professor of Philosophy at the Southern California Institute of Architecture. His most recent books are *Art and Objects* and *Skirmishes*.

OWEN HATHERLEY is the author of several books, including *Red Metropolis* and *Clean Living Under Difficult Circumstances*. He is the culture editor of *Tribune*.

CHRISTIAN W. HOWELL is a Sage Creek High School honors English student. Poetry from his book *13 Things I Love* has been reviewed by Quincy Troupe.

PATRICK A. HOWELL is a poet and entrepreneur at the verbs "do" and "love"... in no particular order. He is the author of *Dispatches from the Vanguard*.

JOE KENNEDY is a writer and lecturer who has published two Repeater books, *Games Without Frontiers* and *Authentocrats*.

MATTEO MANDARINI is Lecturer in Politics and Organisation at Queen Mary University of London and is presently working on a book, *Echoes of Conflict*.

CARL NEVILLE is a writer and critic who lives in London. His most recent work is the critical utopian novel *Eminent Domain*.

ALEX NIVEN lectures at Newcastle University and is the author of *New Model Island*.

MAT OSMAN is an author and musician.

ANDY SHARP is a writer and multimedia artist. An anthology of his work, *The English Heretic Collection*, was published by Repeater in 2020. He lives in London.

CHRISTIANA SPENS is the author of *Shooting Hipsters*, *The Portrayal and Punishment of Terrorists in Western Media* and the forthcoming *The Fear*.

JOY WHITE is a lecturer, writer, and researcher. She is the author of *Urban Music and Entrepreneurship* and *Terraformed: Young Black Lives in the Inner City*.

REPEATER BOOKS

is dedicated to the creation of a new reality. The landscape of twenty-first-century arts and letters is faded and inert, riven by fashionable cynicism, egotistical self-reference and a nostalgia for the recent past. Repeater intends to add its voice to those movements that wish to enter history and assert control over its currents, gathering together scattered and isolated voices with those who have already called for an escape from Capitalist Realism. Our desire is to publish in every sphere and genre, combining vigorous dissent and a pragmatic willingness to succeed where messianic abstraction and quiescent co-option have stalled: abstention is not an option: we are alive and we don't agree.